More Praise for *Beating the Odds*

"Secrets—as only women can share—to advancing and accelerating your career in STEM. Whether it's the good ol' boy network, the glass ceiling, or a lack of role models, *Beating the Odds* shows you how to smash through the barriers that prevent women from a successful career in STEM."

> Elaine Biech, Math Geek and Author, *The New Business of Consulting*

"*Beating the Odds* tells it like it is to be a woman in the tech world. Better, the book tells how to succeed in that world. It's an inspiration."

> Richard A. Moran, PhD., Author, *Sins and CEOs*, President Emeritus, Menlo College

"The ability to tap into the potential of a diverse workforce is a competitive differentiator for innovation and in the technology sector, innovation is king. *Beating the Odds* is a collection of diverse career journeys that provide insightful exploration into what women in technology face through engaging stories and what organizations can do to build a more inclusive and engaging culture."

> David W. Kim, Head of Inclusion & Diversity, Gilead Sciences

"This is a must-read book for those who run businesses and wonder why they can't improve their financial outcomes. *Beating the Odds* is a wake-up call for organizations who have been losing the valuable skills of technical women for decades, and now realize the need to retain and promote them in order to maximize opportunities to grow, profit and innovate. This book helps us understand women's stories, struggles and triumphs in a way that can help C-level and technical executives recognize their own organizational short-comings and align their companies' upward progress with those of women who aspire to and excel in senior-level roles."

> Lisa Suennen, Managing Partner, Venture Valkyrie, LLC, Founder, CSweetener, Women in Healthcare Mentoring

"As technology becomes more critical to corporations, women and (men) who can translate technology into business strategies will be the leaders of the future. *Beating the Odds* tells the powerful stories of how women in STEM are using business acumen to lead their companies and advance their careers at the same time."

>Kevin Cope – Bestselling author and founder of Acumen Learning

"Utilizing the insights and tools provided through compelling stories, the most effective organizations of tomorrow will be led by individuals who read this book TODAY."

>Trent Salvaggio, PhD, Executive Director, IoT Talent Consortium

"A typical 'how-to' self-help book isn't going to inspire women in technical roles to become powerful leaders, however, the inspiring stories of other women, as presented in *Beating the Odds*, is exactly what's needed to instill the confidence women need to become corporate leaders. I plan to share *Beating the Odds* with female engineers whom I provide executive coaching, to help them build the confidence they need to succeed."

>Anthony Fasano, P.E., Bestselling author of *Engineer Your Own Success*, Founder of Engineering Management Institute

BEATING
THE ODDS

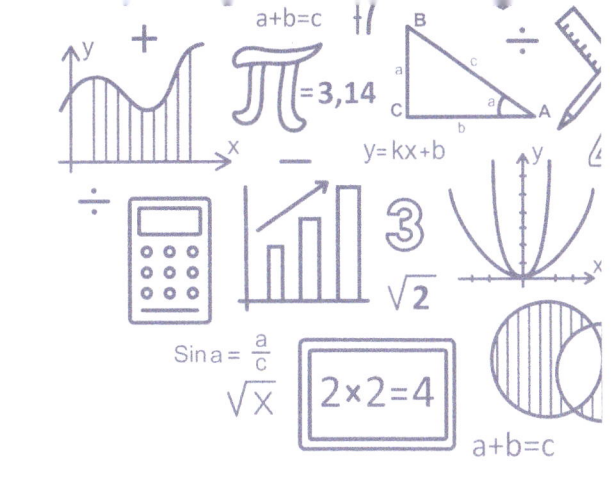

BEATING THE ODDS

Winning Strategies of Women in STEM

Patty Rowland Burke
Kelly Simmons

©2020 Center for Creative Leadership

All Rights Reserved. No part of this publication may be reproduced, stored in a retrieval system, or transmitted, in any form or by any means, electronic, mechanical, photocopying, recording, or otherwise, without the prior written permission of the publisher.

978-1-60491-984-4 – Print

978-1-60491-986-8– Ebook

CCL No. 001009

Published by the Center for Creative Leadership
CCL Press

Authors: Patty Rowland Burke, Kelly Simmons

Editor: Shaun Martin

Rights and Permissions: Kelly Lombardino

https://www.ccl.org/permission-republish-request/

Design and Layout: Carly Bell, Mahmoud Ali

Contents

Preface and Acknowledgments vii

Introduction 1

Geek Girls: Follow Your Calling 7

What Glass Ceiling? 27

Crashing the Good Old Boys' Party 45

Bringing a Business Perspective 67

The Buddy System: Allies and Mentors 85

Generation Next 103

References 119

About the Authors 127

About CCL Women's Leadership 129

About CCL 133

Preface

The seeds for *Beating the Odds* were planted in 2015, when we (Patty and Kelly) met during our first few weeks in our new jobs with the Center for Creative Leadership (CCL). As Kelly was preparing to speak at the Institute of Electrical and Electronics Engineers (IEEE) Women in Engineering (WIE) conference for the 3rd time, we found ourselves evolving a brainstorming of ideas based on our experience regarding the challenges of women in engineering. We started the conversation that turned into a journey about how we at the Center for Creative Leadership could support technical women, such as those at the conference, as they faced similar challenges.

We met with women from WIE Silicon Valley to hear their ideas. We dug through reams of research, some of which showed that while women made up 57 percent of professional positions, they only occupied 27 percent of similar positions in STEM. And 56 percent of those women left their STEM positions at mid-career levels, after 10-20 years (Ashcraft, McLain, & Eger, 2016).

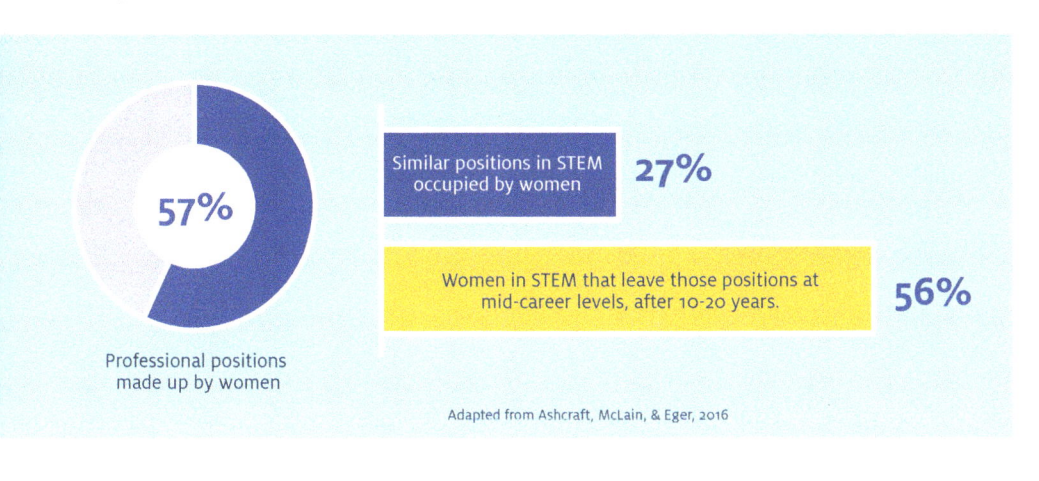

57% Professional positions made up by women

27% Similar positions in STEM occupied by women

56% Women in STEM that leave those positions at mid-career levels, after 10-20 years.

Adapted from Ashcraft, McLain, & Eger, 2016

We explored those findings with WIE members and tested some of the concepts developed from those conversations at their International Leadership Conference. In response to what we were hearing from women engineers in our conversations, we kicked off the first iteration of what was to become Advancing Technical Women in partnership with IEEE WIE. A few months later, we worked with those first attendees and CCL experts to turn those early experiences into what became Advancing Technical Women workshops in 2018.

Learning from Colleagues and Friends

At that point, we drew on our long careers working with technical women to develop the concept of *Beating the Odds*. Kelly drew from her history as a manufacturing engineer, with assignments in Asia and Latin America. When Kelly moved to Spain, she also moved from the engineering field into leadership and organizational development becoming a consultant and eventually an associate coach for CCL in Spain. Upon her return to the United States in 2015, that work merged with supporting tech companies and technical women leaders to grow their leadership impact at a time where tech companies were not investing significantly in their development.

Before joining CCL in 2015, I (Patty) spent my entire career in Silicon Valley as a marketing leader and corporate innovation consultant. In that STEM-driven environment, most of my bosses and clients have been engineers and scientists, and I count many engineers among my friends. As a marketing leader for tech companies, I was constantly on watch for brilliant talent, always looking for people I could draft from engineering departments for my product management and field sales engineering roles. I found it particularly easy to poach women from those engineering roles. In fact, they often came to me.

What this Book Focuses On

We think it's important that the stories and experiences of technical women be told, and we made that the focus of this book. That means there are topics concerning women in the workplace—important topics—that we did not address. We didn't write the book from a general perspective, but from a specific focus on STEM fields and the challenges women face there. Some of these challenges are common with those that women in other workplaces face, such as the struggle to balance work with personal/family life. Many of these common topics are covered well in other books and media, and we encourage you to take advantage of those sources for guidance and insight into issues that we don't cover in *Beating the Odds*.

Although we discuss the exclusion, bias, and hazing that can be directed at women in STEM workplaces, we didn't cover the subject of sexual misconduct (although a couple of the stories we present are examples of it). In the wake of #MeToo, we felt that here, too, the topic is covered well in other media. We strongly support the movement against sexual harassment as we support movements of social justice in general, especially those dealing with gender bias on the individual and cultural level. We acknowledge that there are issues facing women in workplaces other than STEM. We join the efforts of women (and of men) in those workplaces to create more equity and diversity in organizational life.

We hope that our focus on a specific kind of work and its accompanying challenges is a plus for this book. For those technical women who work with us during our Advancing Technical Women programs, the book serves as a companion—although we believe it's helpful on its own. Advancing Technical Women currently runs globally in organizations that seek to develop and bolster their pipeline of STEM women.

Acknowledgments

Just like it takes a village to raise a geek girl, it took a village to make this book happen, and it was an exciting place to live this past year. There are many people to acknowledge, but most importantly, we want to thank the 25 women we interviewed. These women bared their souls, in many cases recalling incidents they had tried to forget, as well as many they were proud to remember. Their excitement about the unique career journeys of women in STEM confirmed that there was a need for this book. We are also grateful to the hundreds of technical women we have known and worked with over the years. They all contributed to our knowledge and passion for telling the stories of women in STEM.

This book wouldn't have been possible without our CCL community of supporters and advisers. Jennifer Martineau, author of *Kick Some Glass* and leader of CCL's equity, diversity, and inclusion practice, was an inspiration, from her Women RISE program to her support of women's research and programs globally. She was also one of our most astute reviewers. Felecia Calloni and Amanda Fonorow provided us with invaluable research assistance. We also thank our other contributors and reviewers, starting with Mary Abraham, who provided another female engineer perspective, and Samir Mehta, Lynn Fick-Cooper, Karissa McKenna, Jennifer Habig, and JaRae Birkeland.

We are forever grateful to Stephanie Trovas. Stephanie fanned the flames of our enthusiasm, from when we began to develop the Advancing Technical Women's program through the writing of Beating the Odds. She motivated us when we were in the doldrums, helped us see the big picture when we were caught in the details, and forced us to focus and get this dang book done! Stephanie was also our partner, supporter and advisor, facilitating the first pilot of Advancing Technical Women, and shepherding it through to completion. She has also been a friend and mentor during our time at CCL, and we love her.

No acknowledgement is complete without thanking the editor, and we had a great one. Pete Scisco was our guiding light. We brought him back from retirement to edit this book, and I know he thought it was worth it. Retirement is overrated! We also want to thank Shaun Martin, Pete's co-editor, who came back from paternity leave to wrap up the book, and Rebecca Addison for providing writing assistance on an early draft and helping us really get started crafting this book. It was a real team effort.

I (Patty) would like to thank my parents, Ron and Bobbie Rowland, who taught me the amazing power of persistence and determination that characterize the women in this book. They are both still striving and persisting in their 90s today.

I (Kelly) want to make a special acknowledgement to Tom Iaia, who infused my first days at HP with the belief that learning and risk taking were the two fundamental features of a first time manufacturing engineer, and that mentoring was a right and not a choice. Beyond enabling the best start to a career I could have ever hoped for, he helped plant the seed that led to me to where I am today.

Introduction

This book chronicles the experiences of technical women in the workplace. The stories of these women are different and include many more challenges than those of women in other roles. People in all kinds of organizational positions who identify as women—from marketing to sales to HR to finance—have workplace challenges. They are often in the minority and experience bias, both conscious and unconscious. But the career of a technical woman adds a twist: she is almost always the "only woman in the room" and often feels isolated and discouraged in an environment dominated by men. Many of these obstacles don't manifest when they embark on a career or enter higher education. They start in grade school.

Those facts and the stories behind them hit us directly during one of the first iterations of CCL's Advancing Technical Women in 2018. We had recruited a group of senior technical women for a dinner panel. Our first surprise was to find out how few of the companies we contacted had technical women in senior positions. The second surprise was the elated reactions of the women in our classroom when they heard about the career journeys of these senior women. Most had never known a woman a senior technical role, much less had a technical woman role model or mentor. They were ravenously hungry for the insights these senior women offered and hung onto their every word. They practically followed them to the elevator and out to the parking lot. The women we had on our panel were not only survivors, they were triumphant. They held leadership positions in world-class companies and managed teams of engineers and scientists on critical projects. It was then we realized that despite the ongoing coverage and analysis of the plight of women in the workplace, the stories of technical women and how they "beat the odds" had not been told often or loud enough.

These Stories Matter

Beating the Odds is a book of stories. Whether you're a senior leader trying to retain technical women, an engineering HR manager trying to support them, or a diversity and inclusion leader trying to change the culture, we hope you will learn from these women and their stories. If you're a woman or student in STEM, we know you will benefit from these amazing and inspiring role models. To quote Roy Peter Clark's *Writing Tools*, "Reports convey information. Stories create experience. Reports transfer knowledge. Stories transport the reader, crossing boundaries of time, space, and imagination. The report points us there. The story puts us there." An advertising executive put it more succinctly: "Facts tell. Stories sell."

While writing this book, we've learned what makes successful technical women tick, why some of them persevere to lead major technical organizations and teams, and why others drop out in frustration. Our journey has led us to look back on the many technical women we have known and worked with over the course of our careers and to reflect on the turning points and pivots in our own careers that ultimately led us to where we are today.

This book puts you in the shoes of women who have risen to success in STEM fields. It will demonstrate, so that you can experience (if you haven't already), the frustrating barriers these women find in the workplace. Barriers that those of us who support their advancement are too familiar with. A senior technical woman should not be an astonishing exception. But we have a long way to go to get there, and this book is our contribution to making that a reality. It should also be noted that this book focuses on the journeys of those who identify as women in technology. We imagine that many similar challenges are faced by individuals who identify as non-binary, agender, gender fluid, etc. However, such comparisons are outside the scope of this book.

Beating the Odds builds on what we both have learned about technical women and tells the stories of women engineers and scientists who beat the odds to advance to director, vice president, or C-level engineering and scientific positions. These women are not necessarily superstars or tech entrepreneurs: most are working engineers and scientists. The women whose stories we tell come primarily from the United States and Europe. They represent a range of technical industries and companies, from cloud computing to mining to pharmaceuticals. While the book builds on insights from hundreds of women, we selected 25 for deeper interviews. All interviewees self-identified as women, therefore, we will be using the terms "woman/women" and pronouns "she/her" throughout this book. Their stories are featured in the pages that follow.

A STEM Woman's Journey

Each chapter in Beating the Odds identifies and explores a common theme arising from our interviews and interactions with women in STEM. Each theme marks the personal histories, examples, and strategies that have helped these women advance in their careers. Our vision was to take readers on a journey with these women as they pursued their careers over years, sometimes decades, identifying critical turning points that make or break their careers. Their experiences are viewed in the context of current events and are informed by research. Each chapter concludes with reflections on those themes and tools for putting insight into action—for individual readers and those who support their efforts and for organizations, as well as those responsible for developing and retaining technical women on their teams and in their companies.

We have used pseudonyms for some of the women whose stories we tell, at their request. We have also used industry descriptions rather than actual company names. With this discretion we gave our interviewees control over how they wanted us to present their experiences. Still, the experiences are real and the women we talked to spoke to us with great passion about their work, their successes and failures, and the lessons they learned in becoming successful in a number of technical fields.

> **Geek girls: follow your calling.** Technical women often start by identifying as "geeks' at an early age. They know without a doubt what they want to be when they grow up. In this chapter, we look at how these girls and young women learn about the importance of identity and how they overcome biases and discouragement, even from the educators who should be encouraging them. Women in this chapter tell how critical the support of parents, particularly mothers, becomes in helping them achieve extraordinary goals.

> **What glass ceiling?** In this chapter, we talk to women who lead major initiatives at the highest levels of their organizations. Many of these women don't believe the glass ceiling exists, or they choose to ignore it. Their successes come from an intense competitive spirit and a laser focus on goals. They accept and revel in the need to be overprepared and "better than" their peers, dismissing the biases and smashing through any barriers they encounter along the way.

> **Crashing the good old boys' party.** Technical women are almost always the "only woman in the room." The women whose stories appear in this chapter are determined to endure and overcome often hurtful hazing, earning the respect of their detractors. They are amazingly resilient and embrace the strategy that what doesn't kill you makes you stronger in order to emerge triumphant from hazing and short circuit attempts to exclude them from important work.

> **Bringing a business perspective.** Women who leapfrog the management hierarchy and earn promotions over men understand the business impact of technology. In this chapter we learn how they use their technical

and scientific knowledge to achieve business goals. An unbeatable combination of business acumen and technical knowledge, particularly in today's tech-driven environments, makes them indispensable contributors to their companies.

The buddy system: allies and mentors. Technical women know it "takes a village" to succeed, and men are important players in that village. Successful technical women often form alliances with men having complementary skills, supporting one another as they move up in their careers. Mentors help women take advantage of stretch assignments and opportunities that they otherwise might miss.

Generation next. Many of the women we interviewed for this book are from the Baby Boomer and GenX generations, who fought their battles before the current awareness and focus on women's leadership and the #MeToo movement. They are now learning from Millennial and GenZ women and supporting their values of equity and transparency. While the entire culture of STEM hasn't shifted, the responses of new generations of women engineers to that culture have changed. These younger women see no reason to put up with exclusion, hazing, or any other gender-biased behaviors and assumptions. And they aren't afraid to speak up about it. They are doing their part to make it possible for technical women to succeed in STEM careers without facing the daunting odds that have historically defined it.

Beating the Odds aims to inspire and empower, and we hope that readers will recognize themselves and take something away from these stories. During a time when Hollywood is creating a stream of blockbuster tales of superheroes, we wanted to find the superpowers that women used to succeed despite the odds. What we found was clarity of purpose and indefatigable perseverance—two pretty good superpowers for the battles they fight.

Still, it would be less than honest to say anything but that careers for women in STEM are still a mixed bag. For every inspiring story, there is a depressing one. There are rarely clear and easy solutions. Our hope is that Beating the Odds will help women and their supporters better understand what's broken in the workplace into which technical women willingly and passionately enter and develop new strategies to fix it. We have seen incredible advances and changes in the year that we have spent researching Beating the Odds, and we hope this book will help accelerate those changes in the days and years to come.

GEEK GIRLS: FOLLOW YOUR CALLING

"No one will really be free until nerd persecution ends." Patrick Henry it's not. But at that moment, the character Gilbert Lowell in *Revenge of the Nerds* anticipates technology's pervasive influence on daily lives around the world. From Instagram updates to mobile phone banking, all kinds of people—from college students to Nairobi shopkeepers—depend on technology for all kinds of activities. It's difficult to imagine a world without the devices we depend on or the systems, like supersized passenger jets, we often take for granted. The nerds are triumphant. Geeks rule.

But while that's a convenient meme and recognizable identity, it wasn't always that way. For example, in 1984, when Gilbert Lowell made his clarion call, many students—at least in the United States—were ridiculed for being academically smart. In those days, geekiness was not cool. That went double for girls. Who can forget Mattel's Teen Talk Barbie's 1992 head-slapping exclamation: "Math class is tough!" Playtime aside, these days women still have a lot of ground to cover. According to the U.S. Department of Commerce, women filled 47 percent of all U.S. jobs in 2015 but held only 24 percent of STEM jobs. Likewise, women constitute slightly more than half of college-educated workers but makeup only 25 percent of college-educated STEM workers (Noonan, 2017).

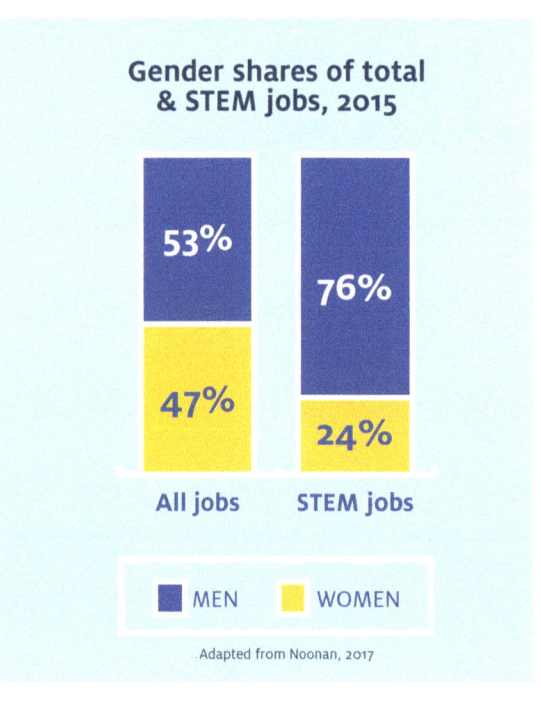

And those disappointing figures are only for the United States, one of the most technologically advanced countries in the world.

But don't tell Rosie Cross that (she already knows). She

Gender shares of total & STEM jobs, 2015

All jobs: MEN 53%, WOMEN 47%
STEM jobs: MEN 76%, WOMEN 24%

Adapted from Noonan, 2017

flipped the script on those profoundly misconceived notions about girls, women, math, and technology. Rosie adopted terms like *nerd* and *geek*, once associated with the unfashionable or socially inept, for her own purposes and put them to work engaging and empowering women to take on the challenges of tech careers. In Australia in 1993, Rosie launched *GeekGirl*, a cyberfeminist digital magazine (now a blog) that married the word *geek* (a word re-popularized in the dot-com era) to her passion for getting more women involved in tech. The magazine was joined by the Girl Geek Academy, which states on its website that it wants to help "one million women to learn technology by 2025".

Geeks are people who go the extra mile to pursue their technical and scientific passions, whether it's *Star Trek*, *Star Wars*, or coding in R. And in 2010 at San Diego Comic-Con International, a panel entitled "Geek Girls Exist" showed widespread recognition of "geek girls" as a community. Geek girls who were once seen as outliers were moving mainstream. In this chapter we focus on how women at an early age recognize their aptitude and passion for science, technology, engineering, and math and learn to embrace their inner geek, and how they build successful careers in technical fields from those beginnings.

Geeks and The Parents Who Launch Them

We imagine Anita Borg would prefer to be known as geek girl as well as a trailblazer, a term often used next to her name. While forging a successful career in computer science, Borg dedicated her energy to fight for greater representation of women in computer and related fields. In 1997 she founded the Institute for Women and Technology (anitab.org since 2018) with the goal of achieving 50 percent representation for women in computing by 2020. We're not there yet, but the work continues. It flows from a strong vision that included Anita's work in computer science and her passion for advancing a common cause for all women in STEM: "We envision a future where the people who imagine and build technology mirror the people and societies for whom they build it." She shared her story in 2003, two years before her death, and it's recorded in the Institute of Electrical and Electronics Engineers (IEEE) History Center. She talked about how her early interest in engineering and science was nurtured by parents who gave her the support she needed to thrive.

"Their attitude about life was always that you should have a good time. My sister and I feel absolutely blessed that we had parents that way. We both went in really different directions, but we both wound up really adventurous about what we did. They taught us that we could do anything we wanted, and if we failed, well, what the heck? You try something else. And that was always the attitude that they had. They never pushed us into anything in particular, but told us if you want to do it, try it; what the heck" (Oral-History, 2001).

Borg believed in advocating for women because she knew the power of advocacy firsthand from her family experience. Supportive parents are a common theme in the lives of many successful technical women. According to our interviews with women in STEM fields, parental encouragement, combined with an early aptitude and love for science and technology, is part of the formula for success in what has traditionally been an industry dominated by men. Taken together, these two factors support many women in overcoming gender barriers during childhood and throughout their careers.

It Takes a Village to Nurture a Girl Geek

Support from parents and mentors at an early age is often the primary factor that propels women into technical fields from which they have been excluded. Research backs this claim. In 2012, research conducted by Jonathan

M. Kane and Janet E. Mertz indicated that in geographical areas where there is gender equity, and where women are making equal pay to men, there is greater performance in math scores by children, with insignificant difference between genders. Their research indicates that having one parent or guardian work in STEM (science, technology, engineering or math) fields makes it more likely for girls to perform better in math and to enroll in a "hard sciences" college degree in programs such as engineering, architecture, math and computer science. This research endorses the idea that an equitable workplace will help advance the academic level of children who are the pipeline to the future workplace.

We first met Nita, a senior engineering director for a major defense company, during the inaugural session of the International Leadership Conference, held for IEEE Women in Engineering (WIE)—the largest engineering membership organization in the world. The 2014 two-day conference in San Jose was the first. Four hundred women attended that year, more than 800 the second year, and the conference continues to grow and prosper, attracting an all-gender crowd and an impressive cadre of speakers and panels on technical and leadership subjects.

When we sat down with Nita five years after she founded the IEEE WIE International Women's Leadership Conference (ILC), she left no doubt about the powerful role her parents played in helping her direct her strengths and

> Having one parent or guardian work in STEM... makes it more likely for girls to perform better in math and to enroll in a "hard sciences" college degree in programs such as engineering, architecture, math and computer science (Kane & Mertz, 2012)

passion toward a career that dove deep into engineering and spread into volunteerism.

"My parents encouraged me to be inquisitive," she said. "With my questions, they encouraged me to become more open minded and more curious. While I had an early interest in technology, it wasn't limited to that. I loved non-technical things, like crafts, and my mother encouraged that. During our summers, we were required to come up with a complex project or challenge to work on. My mom would buy us materials and we would spend our days working on, building, sewing—anything that required coming up with a solution. I loved it. Through these years and summers, I learned that biology did not interest me, but technology did. My parents would always ask me, 'What are you learning? It is not good enough to be better than the bad, you have to strive for goodness on its own.'"

In 2019, at the 6th edition of the International Leadership Conference (ILC), IEEE-USA president Thomas Coughlin shared an impassioned vision for a STEM field beyond gender boundaries. He acknowledged that the movement, so many years in the making, including the ILC spearheaded by Nita, played a crucial role in addressing the issue of gender relations and second-generation bias in STEM. What he, along with many others, struggled with was really understanding the deep seated reasons why it persisted, despite the attention and resources spent to counter it.

Rocking the Science Fair

When Heather was a young girl, her mother went back to school to earn a technical certificate that let her work as a technician at a local gas company. And when Heather decided to build a robot for her third-grade science fair project, her mom was all in. She took Heather to the local Radio Shack where they bought a motor, lights, switches, cables and other equipment. The robot, named Angie, had a plastic milk jug for a body, hair made of yarn, and painted nose and eyes. Angie could move forward and backwards haltingly in a sort of primitive dance. It was a far cry from today's robotics, but it won the science fair, giving Heather the confidence she needed to continue along her technical path.

Not all girls have a mother who works in a technical field. But there are other ways to motivate girls to pursue careers in STEM. As in Heather's case, youth competitions like science fairs give girls the necessary encouragement to pursue their passions. I (Patty) experienced something similar when competing in my own third grade science fair as a girl living in Texas.

I was a marine biology geek from an early age (although I didn't have that language back then). I was totally engrossed in collecting and identifying shells and other objects I gathered from the beach whenever family vacations took us to the Gulf Coast. I even spent my vacation money buying unusual tropical shells at the local tourist shops. Back at home, I spent hours in the library researching scientific names, geographic locations, and other information on habitats of those creatures who once inhabited the shells I collected. My impressive collection ultimately secured my 1st Place ribbon at the school science fair.

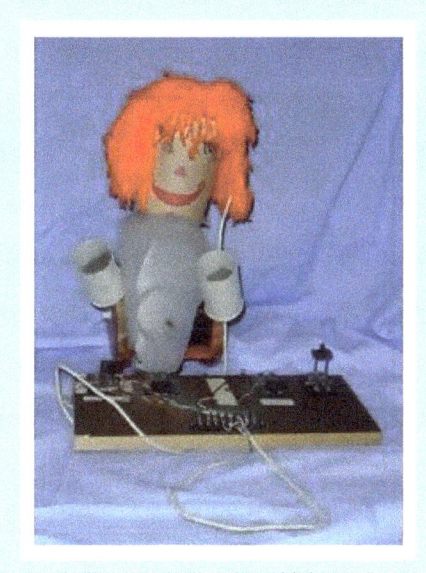

Angie the robot wins the science fair for Heather.

My parents encouraged my passion for science. They gave me a microscope for Christmas one year, and they let me set up a lab in the attic. I spent hours looking at creek water under the microscope, collecting tadpoles and studying their transformation into baby frogs. I excelled in an advanced biology course in high school, but I struggled with math. When it came time for college, I initially decided to major in zoology, but changed majors once I found out about the math requirements. I had bought into the myth that "girls can't do math." My science career was derailed and I ended up in technology marketing with a long-lasting appreciation and envy for women in STEM. I now fulfill my marine biology passion by working with girls in STEM and volunteering at the Monterey Bay Aquarium, but I sometimes wonder what might have been if I hadn't let that stereotype influence me.

Girls *Can* Do Math

Today, math, science and engineering high school classrooms are close to 50-50 boys and girls, a huge step forward from decades earlier. Girls score almost identically to their boy classmates on standardized tests, according to data compiled by the National Girls Collaborative Project, a nonprofit funded in part by the National Science Foundation (Halpern, 2004).

And yet, STEM graduates are still disproportionately men. Men make up 60 percent of the graduates of some fields, and it rises to 80 percent in fields like electrical and mechanical engineering or information technology. What happens? What shifts a girl or woman's perspective on whether to pursue and stick with a career in STEM?

Virginia, a vice president of engineering at a medical device company, heard the same myths as Patty. "I was also told repeatedly that girls are not good at math," she says. "Yet I was always the top of my class and loved it.

That negativity would have been really hard to overcome if I wasn't as good as I was, and that this criticism didn't resonate. It just didn't make sense, so I just decided to ignore it."

Reflecting on her experience, Virginia worries that girls today don't have it any easier. "I still see this with my daughter. There are only a handful of girls taking physics and she still gets explicit and subconscious signals that she does not belong with the top STEM students. It takes me back to when I was in school. Those types of implicit barriers are even harder to fight than the explicit ones," she says.

> Girls score almost identically to their boy classmates on standardized tests, according to data compiled by the National Girls Collaborative Project, a nonprofit funded in part by the National Science Foundation (Halpern, 2004).

The "girls can't do math and science" myth still exists, although it's more limited than in the past. What does continue to keep girls from pursuing STEM careers is a perception of a lack of role models. The STEM fields do not sound appealing or interesting. Over the years, men have defined the terminology and descriptions of the field. Girls simply do not see themselves represented in STEM, and therefore don't see a safe place to try, experiment, fail, and learn (Hill, Corbett, & Rose, 2010).

But the landscape is changing. Every day more organizations and groups of geek girls emerge, serving a critical role in creating a space for women to both find and connect with other women in STEM. Most importantly, they are creating spaces where girls interested in technology can learn, think, and grow together, building an image of a world of women in STEM that is attractive to young girls everywhere.

Geek Girls, Make Your Mark – Redefine the Meme

Beyond the familiar stereotypes, there are many other reasons girls have felt excluded from STEM fields at an early age. While some attitudes, like "girls can't do math," are easy to spot, others are more subtle. Because STEM fields have for so long been dominated by men, exclusion can become embedded even in the work processes and routines that men rarely think about. Riya, an aerospace scientist turned "astroprenuer," discovered some of this hidden bias as a young girl.

Riya was fascinated by space as a girl and closely followed the Apollo missions and the Mars landing. Even though she was very young at the time, she remembers every detail of both with crystal clarity. She says she would look up at the night sky and think to herself, "Yeah, I want to be there. I want to help people fly there."

Classic Spectral Types

- **O B A F G K M**
- (**O**h, **B**e **A** **F**ine **G**irl, **K**iss **M**e!) (mnemonic)
- Spectral type is directly related to temperature
- From O to M, the temperature decreases
- O type, the hottest, blue color, Temp ~ 25000 K
- M type, the coolest, red color, Temp ~ 3000 K
- Sub-classes, e.g. B0, B1...B9, A0, A1...A9
- The Sun is a G2 type of star (temp. 5800 K)

"This all blew my mind. I was completely amazed and enthralled with science and space. In fact, my favorite planet as a kid was Jupiter and I ended up doing my PhD on it," she says. But as a young girl, studying astronomy at the kitchen table, Riya came across the mnemonic for the order of star temperatures: OBAFGKM (Oh Be A Fine Girl Kiss Me).

She was incensed and quickly voiced her frustration to her mother. She still remembers when her mother, dressed in a sari, looked up from the ironing board and calmly responded, "Then why don't you grow up and change it."

Riya describes her mom at the time as a "closet feminist." She says, "It wasn't feasible for my mom to have a career, but she wanted me to do my best to be successful and make a difference." While discovering that mnemonic was a negative experience for Riya, it drove her to achieve her dream of becoming an aerospace scientist. The mnemonic is still in use today, but the words "guy" and "girl" are now used interchangeably.

Women have a long history in astronomy, as reflected in a famous photo of Einstein surrounded by several women at the Yerkes Observatory in Williams Bay, Wisconsin. However, Riya notes that these women were primarily "number crunchers," like the women portrayed in the 2016 film Hidden Figures (Chernin, 2016). She says there are still few women in management at observatories. In fact, only in the last few decades have famous telescope sites such as Caltech's Palomar Observatory near San Diego, California (known as "The Monastery"), smoothed the way for women to use the facilities. Previously on-site housing was only made available to men.

On the international stage, progress is also much in evidence. For example, women engineers played key roles in the Indian Space and Research Organization's (ISRO) maiden mission to Mars (Mangalyaan) in November 2013. Of the 500-member team, women made up 27 percent of the executive level (Bhatti, 2019).

From "You Can't" To "I Can"

Many of the technical women we spoke with experienced plenty

Women at the Yerkes Observatory.

of dismissive and discouraging comments as girls, but they persevered. Francesca, who started her career as a drug development scientist and is now an expert on digital transformation, went to an all-girls Catholic high school in Spain. She says when she told her teachers she was interested in science as a young girl their response was, "Don't be silly. Women can't be scientists."

While we might now see those teacher's remarks as part of the excluding myth in the mold of "girls can't do math," they surprised Francesca. But rather than discourage her, they spurred her to work harder. She dug into science and math, earning excellent grades in these subjects. Still, the attitude persisted through her senior year, when she found out that her school was reluctant to provide her records for applications to technical universities and she had to insist that they send them. "Had I not been stubborn, that would have been the end of the road for a career that has been so personally and professionally satisfying for me," she says.

Immigration and Geek Girls–Coming to America

We talked to many women about how the combination of parental support and persistence led them to stellar careers. The parents who went above and beyond to advocate for their children are especially notable—and integral to their success. These women did not only have strong parental support—their parents were willing to take daring leaps of faith to provide them with the best education and opportunities. In many cases, that meant a journey to the United States.

Christine, now the chief medical officer at a clinical AI company, was inspired by her mother, who had a degree in foreign languages and literature but took night classes in computer science while Christine was growing up in order to get a better job. Christine followed in her footsteps and was an excellent student with a laser focus on math and science. Because Christine grew up in a lower-middle-class family in Minnesota, the University of

Minnesota seemed like the most logical and affordable choice for her college education. However, Christine wanted the chance to attend one of the top technical schools in the United States and decided to apply to only her top two choices, MIT and Stanford, to save money on application fees. She was accepted to both, but when it came time to visit the campuses, her family couldn't afford the travel expenses. Christine was undeterred. She followed the advice of her mother, who said, "If we can move here from Taiwan without visiting first, then you can go to college without visiting first." Through a combination of part-time jobs, scholarships, and loans, Christine went on to earn her computer science and engineering undergraduate, master's, and doctoral degrees from MIT, as well as a PhD from Harvard.

June, who serves as vice president of software engineering at a major cloud services company, took an even greater leap of faith, moving from a small village in China to Alabama, sight unseen. Her family's circumstances could have derailed her young dreams, but her parents recognized her passion and technical aptitude and supported her education from the beginning.

When June first started school at five years old she was already demonstrating abilities at the third-grade level and her success only continued from there. Her persistence and her aptitude in math led her to earn an undergraduate degree in computer science at Beijing University. A full scholarship to the University of Alabama in the United States followed.

To send June there, her father sold everything he owned and bought her a one-way ticket to Alabama. For a young country girl who barely spoke English and had never been on a plane, she initially experienced intense culture shock. However, June quickly mastered English, worked as a research assistant, and began publishing in her field. She ultimately earned a PhD in computer science and was the only woman in her graduating class.

Like June, Neetu and her sister also immigrated to the United States to pursue higher education. Her parents were proud of their girls and gave their daughters every advantage they could afford. At the age of four, Neetu was sent to a competitive English-speaking immersion school. She was an excellent student overall, excelling in science, math, and chemistry. She especially loved problem solving. "It wasn't memorization," Neetu says. "I really had a creative approach to solving problems and I loved it"

Neetu's four male cousins were all good in math and became engineers. She decided she would do the same, particularly since it required less time than studying to become a doctor (her second choice). She became the first woman engineer in her extended family. But the road there wasn't without challenges. For example, Neetu didn't own a computer, and she was constantly in the library or school using their computers. Her supportive family, friends and teachers always ended up finding a way to get her the tools she needed. "People were so supportive," she says. "Everyone saw something in me and helped me out and helped me push beyond my boundaries."

After earning her undergraduate degree from the SGS Institute of Science and Technology in India, Neetu received a full scholarship to the University of Cincinnati and began her career as an engineer. She now leads hardware engineering teams at one of the largest technology companies in the world.

Owning the Geek Thing

The women we interviewed would not have benefited from the support of their parents and others without already possessing a burning passion for science and technology at an early age. Research shows that women who believe that being an engineer is an intrinsic part of their identity will tend to stay in that field longer than 15 years, which is when many women leave the field (Ramsey & McCorduck, 2005).

Take Lisa's story as an example. An industrial engineer and CEO of a medical device company, Lisa has been proud of her identity throughout her life. "I always owned the 'geek' thing," she says. "In fact, I got the 'pink protractor' award in graduate school. Unlike many girls and women, I never felt like I had to hide it. I was always analytical and knew I wanted to do something with math and science, maybe become a math teacher. There are women who just have that DNA. It serves me well as a CEO today—I can go deep into both the technology and the numbers. Sometimes, women who come from an engineering background and who want to advance can attempt to distance themselves from their own technical background so that they can grow as a business leader and not be put in the 'engineering box,' but I have found, on the contrary, that owning my technical background engenders respect across the board."

Beverly, who earned an undergraduate degree in metallurgical engineering, had a similar experience growing up. "I was a proud geek," she says. "I loved solving problems, analyzing data—I always had an affinity for it. And fortunately, I was raised to ask for what I wanted. I'll never forget my mother saying, 'If you have a college education and work hard, you can rule the world—even in a men's only profession.'"

Follow Your Calling

Lisa and Beverly, like other women we spoke with, found their calling early and embraced it. Research tell us it's the right move. A 2017 research study by CCL and Watermark, a northern California Bay Area women's advocacy group, shows that women want to work for organizations that help them find their calling: Women are drawn to work that is personally meaningful, fits well with their lives and their values, and is enjoyable (Clerkin, 2017).

Job fit and enjoyable work are the two biggest reasons employees stay with their organizations.

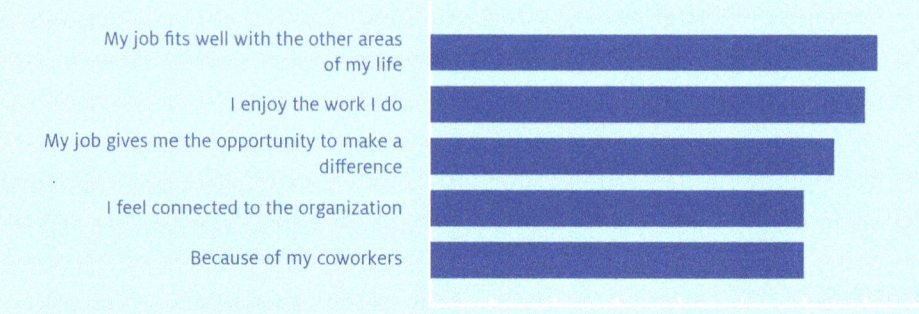

- My job fits well with the other areas of my life
- I enjoy the work I do
- My job gives me the opportunity to make a difference
- I feel connected to the organization
- Because of my coworkers

Adapted from American Psychological Association. (2012, August 28). Work-life fit and enjoying what they do top the list of reasons why employees stay on the job, new APA survey finds [Blog post]. Retrieved from http://www.apa.org/news/press/releases/2012/08/work-life.aspx

Similarly, according to a report published in *Educational Psychology Review*, research shows that aptitude and interest are equally crucial to determining the career paths that individuals choose. Girls with high math achievement and little interest or motivation in pursuing a STEM occupation are far less likely to obtain a science degree than individuals with average math skills and high interest in science (Wang & Degol, 2017). It's easy to see from these studies that a unique attribute of successful technical women is their recognizing the need to follow their calling at a young age. With the help of parents and mentors working to dispel gender myths and to guide young girls in the right direction, this calling can become a reality.

Takeaways, Tips, and Tools

- Women in STEM have benefited from trailblazers, who helped transform terminology used in the aerospace workplace from language that subtly reinforces stereotypes to more broadly accessible, gender-neutral, and inclusive language.

- Attracting women to and retaining them in STEM means companies, managers, leaders, policy makers, and colleagues need to evolve how they perceive women and girls in technical fields and how those women and girls perceive themselves.

- The nerds may be having their revenge, but we still need stronger and more supportive connections between geekiness and what is considered cool and creative. All of us can celebrate women's many contributions to technical fields from space discovery to biology to software development.

Here are some things you can do to align with your inner geek. Think about how they (and similar ideas you come up with, perhaps in conversation with a supportive peer, boss, or mentor) can help you build the passion and determination to do whatever is necessary to build and sustain your STEM career.

For those leaders and organizations supporting women in STEM fields, it's about inclusion. Use these lists to create assignments with enough challenge and support. Think of how they might be used in a system-wide developmental strategy.

What You Can Do

Be true to yourself. Is where you are right now aligned with who you are and where you want to be? Is it the right next step on your journey? What helps keep women and girls—and can help you—successfully embrace their inner geek is a sense of identity. Knowing that can guide your choices in how to manage your technical journey.

Make a list of aspects that form your identity. Set aside some time and write down words that describe yourself in the following three categories. Those can include your "given" identity (aspects about you that you had no choice in, example: deaf, or Hungarian parents), "chosen identity" (aspects you have selected yourself, example: engineer, or spouse), and "core" identity (aspects that make you unique and different from others, example: innovator, or energizer). Together, these aspects form your *social identity*. Ask yourself:

- Which aspects of your social identity are most relevant to your present role?

- Which aspects contribute to your current performance?

- Which aspects hinder your current performance?

- Which aspects do you want to make more prominent in future roles?

- Which aspects will you want to tap into more, or tap into less?

Find your tribe. Sebastian Junger (2016) writes that we all yearn to belong to groups that are defined by their purpose and perspective: *tribes*. Look for organizations, associations, and interest groups that support your inner geek. Discovering and helping to build a tribe is a different way to talk about what we normally refer to as *networking*. In CCL's Advancing Technical Women program, the women who attend are usually an even mix between networkers and non-networkers, but women in both groups rarely claim to have found a fulfilling tribe. By the end of the two-day course, where the women work as members of a temporary tribe, they often feel passionately motivated to find a tribe to call their own.

In their book, *Kick Some Glass: 10 Ways Women Succeed at Work on Their Own Terms*, authors Jennifer Martineau and Portia Mount walk through steps you can take to build your network of champions. We highly recommend the book as a resource for STEM women determined to build meaningful networks—to find their tribe. We also include a selection of organizations that appeal to and support geek girls as resources at the end of this book.

What Organizations Can Do

Create and support Employee Resource Groups (ERG). These entities support technical women and geek girls (for schools and other youth-oriented organizations) through the challenges they might face at work and school. A few we know of have been grass roots efforts initiated by technical women on the job. Some companies are providing funds for development directly to these employee lead ERGs. *Working Mother Media* can help you get started with guidelines to best practices. Find them at www.diversitybestpractices.com.

Host events to showcase women in tech. We read LinkedIn daily where, every day, dozens of organizations are showcasing and broadcasting their women in tech. Bring in speakers with successful STEM careers, provide demonstrations of STEM work, organize discussion groups on STEM subjects, and create other gatherings where technical women and the men who support them can share and learn.

Support girls in STEM. Some local educational institutions—high schools, colleges, and universities—welcome corporate involvement with students of all levels. ERGs will often work with local groups to develop STEM support programs. We have seen both scientists and engineers (of all genders) get involved with students, building lifelong relationships and having an enormous impact on their careers.

Take values into account. During talent conversations, ask questions that focus on the employee's personal values. Managers can better support their direct reports when they find roles and assignments that best align with her talents.

WHAT GLASS CEILING?

It is the spring of 1997 in San Jose, California, and a rapt audience of 3,000 women of Hewlett Packard listen to the speaker's tale. It is a story of a woman who chased her dream to work in the technical field—the field of space travel. She takes them on a journey through her career, sharing how her childhood dream of flying to Mars led to her role in helping to land the Sojourner Rover.

The speech intends to give the women in the audience a sense that in their careers, anything is possible. The speech is motivating, but despite the speaker's best intentions, it can't disguise one fact: Ample evidence demonstrates that pervasive barriers still exist for women in STEM. The attrition rate for women in STEM is around 50 percent—an incredible loss of talent (Glass, Sassler, Levitte & Michelmore, 2013).

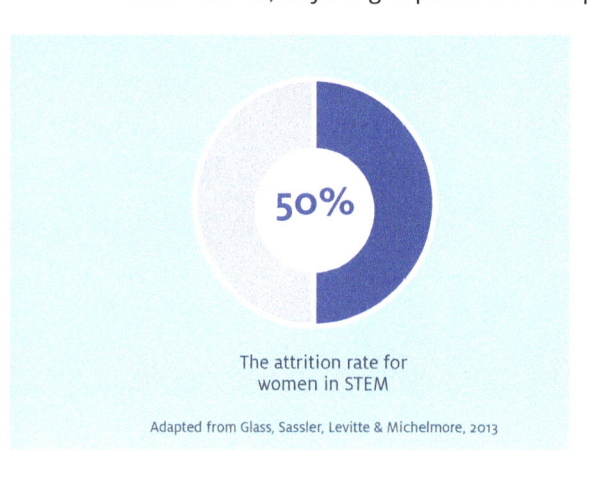

50%

The attrition rate for women in STEM

Adapted from Glass, Sassler, Levitte & Michelmore, 2013

In the high-tech industry, for example, the quit rate for women is 41 percent, compared with 17 percent for men. Similarly, women continue to face salary equity challenges. An analysis of the U.S. Census Bureau's 2013 American Community Survey data found that women in computer and mathematical occupations were paid 87 percent of what men in similar occupations made (Corbett & Hill, 2015).

Most women working in STEM have experienced—or know someone who has experienced—a barrier of some kind, whether overt or not. However, despite the extensive research on the subject and frequent stories in the media, there are some women working in STEM today who say they have never experienced the barriers associated with the phrase glass ceiling.

In this chapter we look at what can be learned from that perspective.

How do the experiences of women who do not perceive a glass ceiling help us make their perception a reality for all women in STEM? Did these women experience barriers that they simply didn't notice? Or, did these women have different advantages that helped mitigate barriers to their work and career? What role does a person's attitude and worldview play in success? If we don't acknowledge the barriers women in STEM face, can we minimize their impact? How can women reframe their experiences to build more successful and fulfilling careers in technical fields?

Eyes on the Prize

When Janis started working at NASA's Jet Propulsion Laboratory (JPL) in 1980, she was the only woman out of 180 engineers in her section. However, being in the minority wasn't new for her. During her time studying aerospace engineering at the University of Toronto, she was one of only a few women in her undergraduate class. Her graduate class of 60 only had two women as well.

"Women today seem more sensitive to their female peer group and notice the number of women," Janis says. "What we have seen is that the ratio of men/women in undergraduate engineering degrees has stayed relatively consistent over the years. What has changed is how aware we are of the statistics in the 2000s as compared with the 70s or 80s."

A lack of gender diversity at JPL didn't seem to faze Janis. She was inspired to join JPL to work on NASA's Galileo mission, launched to study Jupiter and its moons. She didn't stop there. Today, Janis serves as the project manager of the Europa Clipper mission to Jupiter's moon Europa, after recently completing a stint as the director for engineering and science at JPL. "I found four to five male colleagues who became my work peer group," she says. "In

> **The ratio of men/women in undergraduate engineering degrees has stayed relatively consistent over the years. What has changed is how aware we are of the statistics in the 2000s as compared with the 70s or 80s.**

my view, at JPL you were valued for what you brought to the table. I also had male mentors, both early on and throughout my career, and I felt that I was treated as an equal to everyone else."

Despite increases in academic attainment, women still experience a similar environment to Janis's situation and remain underrepresented in STEM careers. According to the National Science Board, while women make up half of the total U.S. college-educated workforce, they represent only 29 percent of the science and engineering workforce (2016).

However, to many women in the fields of mechanical and electrical engineering, it feels normal to work in fields dominated by men. In fact, research shows that most engineers don't perceive bias or barriers at the outset of their careers (Orser, Riding, & Stanley, 2011). This could be because while gender representation in STEM fields has increased in recent decades, our focus as a society on gender equity has also increased.

The Competitive Edge

In a 2014 study published in *Motivation and Emotion*, New York University psychology researchers examined the link between perception and motivation. Specifically, they looked at how focusing on a specific target ahead can make walking as a form of exercise easier. According to their study, people who kept their "eyes on the prize" said the exercise required 17 percent less exertion than those in the baseline group. Additionally, members of the first group walked 23 percent faster (Cole, Riccio, & Balcetis, 2014).

The NYU study suggests an interesting reason driving the success of some technical women. While women entering STEM careers twenty or thirty years ago might have had a harder time breaking the glass ceiling, many who succeeded didn't focus on the barriers preventing them from getting ahead. Instead, these women looked beyond the glass ceiling, keeping their eyes on the prize and focusing on the target ahead.

Many of the women we interviewed revel in success and have used that feeling to push themselves further in their careers. In some cases, competition prompted them to study the very STEM subjects they work in today and in other cases, competition is what propelled them to the forefront of their fields. For her part, when she was young Janis says she had no idea what an engineer was. Her father was a lawyer. She didn't even know what an engineer was. But she knew she enjoyed math and science in high school along with languages. Her father suggested she might become a translator for science journals.

During her senior year in high school Janis dated a boy whose father was an engineer. "He ended up applying to an engineering science program," she says. She might have taken the path her father had suggested, but she says she felt pulled toward being an engineer herself—and excited about the level of competition she might face to make it so. "I felt this pull, away from the career my father had suggested," Janis says. "I realized that somewhere inside, I am more competitive than I originally realized. I came to this conclusion because I literally thought, 'If he can [the boy she had dated] do that, so can I." When Janis applied to the University of Toronto's School of Engineering she was accepted—an important step in her STEM journey.

When we spoke with Prisha, we found her no stranger to "taking on the boys." Her experience reveals how perceptions can shift not only for women but for the men they work with.

"During my studies, I was aware that I liked competing and proving to boys I can be just as good as them. I always wanted to beat the boys and prove that I was as good. And at the same time, I did not feel that there was really an observable gender difference. I saw myself as a competitor among peers. It wasn't until during a machine design course that the idea of gender difference in engineering was brought up. In that course, like many others, there were two girls. I turned to a friend to tell him that I had noticed that there were two girls in this class. He replied, 'I see one. Who is the other?' He didn't even see me as a girl! For me the point was, no one cares. I enjoyed this. I saw it as fun—proof that I can hang, I'm just as good."

What happens to turn a competitive spirit into a perspective that recognizes few if any boundaries? And what is the connection to determination and keeping eyes on the goal? One possibility connecting the two might be that for people who take pleasure from competing successfully create what positive psychology pioneer Mihaly Csikszentmihalyi called flow. He defines flow as a state of complete absorption in which a person feels completely engaged and satisfied and time seems to pass unnoticed.

According to Csikszentmihalyi (1990), "The best moments usually occur when a person's body or mind is stretched to its limits in a voluntary effort to accomplish something difficult and worthwhile. Optimal experience is thus something we make happen" (p. 3). When a person engages in an activity they can do well, time falls away.

The competitive edge they sharpened in school allowed these women to engage deeply in technical subject matter, where at some level, they engaged in a state of flow. In turn, those periods of flow allowed them to excel in their respective fields and ignore the gender barriers that might have held them back. The oscillating engagement and absorption trained their eyes on the road ahead and made them blind (to one degree or another) to gender bias in STEM that could have slowed or stopped their trajectories. Essentially, success breeds success.

Stretch and Support

Have you ever taken on a job or some other task for which you didn't feel ready for? And then when you are successful at handling that challenge, do you remember how energized and confident that made you feel? Many of the women we interviewed for this book began those experiences at a young age. If that describes your experience, reflect on how that feeling of accomplishment might serve as a guiding force, directing you to put yourself in environments where you can continue to excel. Competence can erase gender lines. When women succeed in environments traditionally dominated by men it can be so gratifying as to eliminate perceptions they might have that a gender imbalance exists.

A 2014 *Harvard Business Review* article included the results of a survey which asked 823 international executives what had help them achieve their potential during their careers. Seventy-one percent of respondents but stretch assignments at the top of the list. In second place were job rotations and personal mentors, which were each mentioned by 49 percent of respondents (Fernández-Aráoz, 2014).

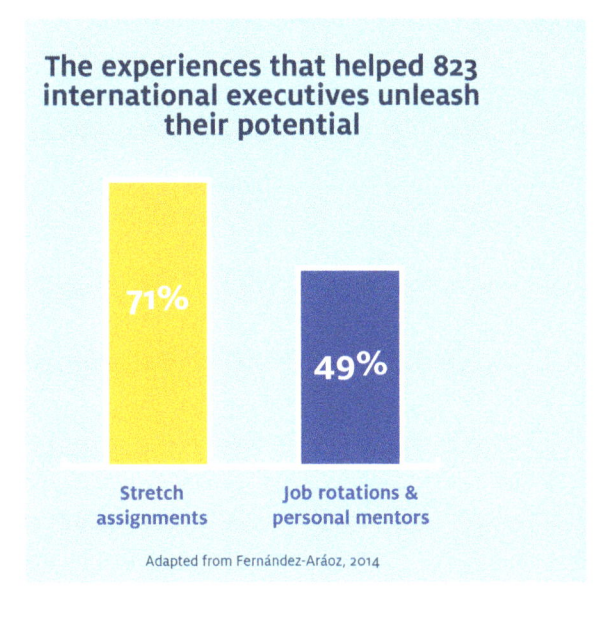

The experiences that helped 823 international executives unleash their potential

- Stretch assignments: 71%
- Job rotations & personal mentors: 49%

Adapted from Fernández-Aráoz, 2014

33

Those three career enablers—stretch assignments, job rotations, and mentors—are especially beneficial to women in STEM. For example, Prisha took advantage of early career job rotations to enable a quick launch to her advancement. Her first role at the organization at which she still works today included a rotation between departments. "When I became a product development team lead, it was then unheard of for someone straight out of school with one year of rotation experience," Prisha says. "Most people with that job had 10-15 years of experience. And immediately, I was working with guys with 30 years design experience and I had to tell them what to do. It was an amazing growth experience."

Prisha's initial experience fueled years of living in continuous stretch. "I've always had jobs that I haven't been qualified for," she says. "I had no experience. I recruited a couple of people who would spend time with me and be my tech experts, and I tried to learn what I thought I needed to know from them."

A 2016 report by the Center for Creative Leadership asserts that challenging assignments make up the largest percentage of key developmental experiences (Gurvis, McCauley, & Swofford). Stretch assignments put individuals in new or uncertain situations where they can build new skill sets and gain deeper expertise. These assignments often include facing unfamiliar or broader responsibilities. Stretch assignments are challenging, but they are manageable. For many women, stretch assignments have a whole different level of difficulty other than the job itself.

Ten Types of Stretch Assignments

	Description	Benefits
Unfamiliar Responsibilities	Handling responsibilities that are new or very different from previous ones you've handled.	Gives you the opportunity to practice new skills and expand your knowledge base.

New Directions	Starting something new or making strategic changes.	Gives you the opportunity to take initiative, explore and create, and organize people to make things happen.
Inherited Problems	Fixing problems created by someone else or existing before you took the assignment.	Gives you the opportunity to tackle problems, diagnose and understand root causes, and reenergize people.
Problems with Employees	Dealing with employees who lack adequate experience, are incompetent, or are resistant to change.	Gives you the opportunity to deal with people problems, face and resolve conflict, and coach employees to higher levels of performance.
High Stakes	Managing work with tight deadlines, pressure from above, high visibility, and responsibility for critical decisions.	Gives you the opportunity to be decisive, work and learn at a fast pace, and have significant impact.
Scope and Scale	Managing work that is broad in scope (involving multiple functions, groups, locations, products, or services) or large in sheer size (e.g., workload, number of responsibilities).	Gives you the opportunity to coordinate and integrate across groups, delegate to others, and create systems to monitor and track work.
External Pressure	Managing the interface with important groups outside the organization, such as customers, vendors, partners, unions, and regulatory agencies.	Gives you the opportunity to represent your organization, to influence and negotiate with external groups, and to build shared agendas among diverse groups.

Influence without Authority	Influencing peers, higher management, or other key people over whom you have no direct authority.	Gives you the opportunity to work across organizational boundaries, coordinate action across the organization, and handle internal politics.
Work across Cultures	Working with people from different cultures or with institutions in other countries.	Gives you the opportunity to become more aware of your own cultural biases, to adapt to different expectations, and to manage across distances.
Work Group Diversity	Being responsible for the work of people of different genders and different racial and ethnic backgrounds.	Gives you the opportunity to work with diverse people, to recognize the need to overcome stereotypes and biases, and to persuade people from different backgrounds to work together.

Adapted from McCauley, 2006

For Janis, the stretch into more responsibility did not come at any expense to her family life. She was able to power down and work part time for about six years while her two children were infants and preschoolers. To power down is one of the two most-used strategies for women looking to sustain their careers while managing time-consuming activities such as childcare or assisting elderly parents. The other most popular strategy is to take on a new career (Martineau & Mount, 2019). Janis chose the former, and she took advantage of available opportunities that allowed her to move her career forward. In the summer of 1996, she was working on the Cassini mission to Saturn when she was asked to return to return to work full time. "I had been the deputy manager on the control system, and my experience lent itself better to the final push of project," Janis says. "When my manager took another job, I came back to be the lead on the project."

After Casini launched, Janis moved into concept design, where she spent three years. But she realized that that phase of project development did not appeal to her or leverage her strengths. She moved to a line management role until she was asked to manage the flight software development for the Mars Rover. "Each request was tapping into the experience I had accumulated over, at that point, 20 years," she says. "My career opportunities broadened from there in both line management and project development roles until I reached the area of spaceflight project management responsibility, the highest level in our line of work. I was asked to take on the role of project manager for the Juno mission, a $1B mission to Jupiter."

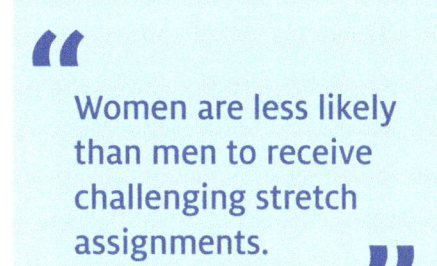

> **Women are less likely than men to receive challenging stretch assignments.**

Stretch assignments are important to development because they help workers access the diverse experiences necessary to develop a broad repertoire of leadership skills. However, despite the power stretch assignments have to fast track a person's career, according to a McKinsey and Company report, women are less likely than men to receive challenging stretch assignments. (Huang, Krivkovich, Starikova, Yee, & Zanoschi, 2019).

The actions of Janis and Prisha demonstrate how certain experiences and attitudes can minimize the impact of the glass ceiling. From an early age neither woman let gender biases dissuade her from pursuing a career in STEM. Instead, they relished the opportunity to compete against the men in their fields. Rather than feeling intimidated, each took advantage of challenging opportunities to spur her forward along her career trajectory. And both had the support necessary to ensure their assignments were worthwhile.

> **While support during stretch assignments can help women manage their careers and advance in their technical field, a lack of support for stretch assignments can contribute to stalling women in technical careers.**

Another factor Janis and Prisha shared was that, during their stretch assignments, neither woman worked alone; they leaned into a cadre of mentors along the way. Mentors have long served as a vital source of leadership development, and they're key to enhancing outcomes from stretch assignments. By accessing stretch assignments and with the help of supportive mentors, Janis and Prisha were able to bypass some of the common barriers women experience in STEM fields.

Mentors not only help women take on the challenges of stretch assignments, they can also help identify developmental experiences in the first place. In our mentoring work with women who have participated in CCL's Advancing Technical Women program, we have seen that many women don't recognize the potential stretch assignments that can make or break a career. Charlotte is a case in point. She was an engineering lead managing a group of eight people at a growing financial services company in San Francisco. She told her mentor how excited the whole company was over its acquisition of a small competitor. The acquired company had several offshore engineering teams. One of these teams had very similar skills and responsibilities as the group that Charlotte managed.

Charlotte told her mentor she was really interested to see who that group will end up reporting to. Her mentor asked the obvious: "Why shouldn't they report to you?" That thought hadn't even crossed Charlotte's mind. Her mentor pointed out that Charlotte was qualified and let her sleep on it a few days. At that point Charlotte was ready to sit with her mentor and develop a strategy about out how she should approach the acquisition team, detailing her qualifications and vision for the group. She was well prepared for the discussion, the acquisition team almost immediately agreed with her argument, and Charlotte was promoted and made team leader for the acquired group, which she has since integrated into her team. "It's definitely a stretch," she says, "but once we talked it through, I realized I was ready for it and was just as qualified as anyone else in the company."

Bounce Back and Forward

While the careers of the women discussed in this chapter seem to consistently move forward, the reality is that career paths seldom make for smooth strolls to the next level. Some women slow down and then speed up. Others bounce backward, getting thrown off track, before moving forward in a new trajectory.

Silvia's story is another look at how a mentor can help keep a career on track. Silvia complained in an email to her mentor about a new assignment from the vice president of her division that she was planning to turn down since she felt it would signal an interest in doing project management instead of more technical, software development work. Her mentor asked that she hold off on her decision until they could talk. What her mentor saw that Silvia hadn't was that the breadth of the assignment provided powerful developmental opportunities for Silvia to demonstrate her leadership skills across the entire organization. Silvia accepted the assignment. In addition to managing the project, she also took the opportunity to build relationships with the heads of the divisions and her colleagues across the organization. Silvia's work led to a promotion, where she was able to select her next assignment.

While support during stretch assignments can help women manage their careers and advance in their technical field, a lack of support for stretch assignments can contribute to stalling women in technical careers. When this happens, the glass ceiling becomes very real and many women slam into it, suffering near career-ending injuries. Riya tells the story that changed the trajectory of her career: "After I had my second child while finishing my PhD, I had an opportunity to work on the Spitzer Space Telescope. I quickly learned when you work with men and have a baby on your hip, so to speak, there is an assumption made that you don't have the commitment to move into management. Decision-making, controlling budgets, that wasn't happening for women. Even though I was more than qualified, I couldn't break into management, I was always viewed as an individual contributor."

The last straw was a project in which she was clearly the most qualified to lead. Riya had the experience and the specific technical background for the high profile, rapid turnaround mission. But the project lead was given instead to a man and she was made his deputy. Riya ended up managing the project anyway when the project leader missed key meetings."I did the agendas, managed the meetings and competed the proposal.Neither of us had experience doing budgets. Senior management assigned someone to help him, which they could easily have done for me."

The final insult, which involved a different project, happened when her supervisor took the marker away from her when she was at the whiteboard during a meeting. "It was clear that he was not convinced that I was capable of executing the project," Riya says. "I just stood there looking confused and a bit astonished at what had just happened. When no one looked uncomfortable, I knew it was time to move on."

Gender biases persist because people have deeply ingrained beliefs and practices that sustain those biases. A recent study published in the *American Educational Research Journal* demonstrates just how pervasive these biases can be (Ganley, George, Cimpian, & Makowski, 2018). According to their research, perceived gender bias in any given discipline is the primary criterion women use for selecting a college major. If young women can already identify careers that are inherently biased, why would any of them even begin to prepare for them? In order to break the glass ceiling, it might be time for women to look past it.

Takeaways, Tips, and Tools

- Many women see a limitless future and have propelled themselves forward at every opportunity in their own unique ways. What makes them different from many women who get stuck in their technical careers is that they perceive choices where others see barriers.

- For women in STEM, growth comes through experience, and seeking or being sought for challenging stretch assignments is critical for growth and advancement.

- Careers rarely follow a straight path. When faced with an insurmountable obstacle or blatant bias, look for another path—even if it means moving to another organization.

Take the following lists as idea starters. Think about how they (and similar ideas you come up with, perhaps in conversation with a supportive peer, boss, or mentor) can help you rise above or around the glass ceilings you encounter. And for people charged with developing women in STEM careers, use these lists to create stretch assignments with enough challenge and support, and think of how those assignments might be used in a systemwide developmental strategy.

What You Can Do

CCL Senior Fellow Cindy McCauley has spent decades studying how leaders develop through their work. Knowing who you are, your values, and goals comes first. After that, creating a plan for development that helps you accomplish the five following tactics will go a long way toward creating a positive career trajectory and escaping from under any barriers that might come along (2006).

Set learning goals. Focus on learning during your experiences and not just on achieving a goal. Ask yourself: What knowledge do I want to acquire? What skills do I want to improve? (Think technical and leadership skills.) What new perspectives do I want to gain? What bad habits do I want to change?

Tap into expertise. Too often, people take on an assignment without thinking about what they need to learn to do it successfully. Capitalize on all the learning that has already happened in the world—don't start with a blank slate! Where can you learn? What topics do you need to be reading about? What training programs will get you ready for a new experience? Who has the expertise that you want to tap into? Who could serve you as a wise counsel?

Experiment and get feedback. From leadership to sports to smoking cessation, behavioral science says that we get better through a process of Action-Reaction-Adjustment. That's what learning from experience is all about! What requires you to experiment to find what works in a new assignment? What might you need to do differently from what you've done in other situations? Who can you enlist to give you useful feedback on how you're doing? What should you track to see how your progressing?

Lean on others. Learning, growth, and change are hard—you will need the support of others! Ask yourself who can be your confidant as you struggle to learn? Who will encourage you and lift your spirits when the going is tough? Who understands you enough to see through your excuses and procrastinations? Who do you want as company on your learning journey?

Take time to reflect. The most undervalued tool at your disposal might be your ability to expand your mindset. Don't just go through a new experience—absorb it! Take time to think about your approach, your actions, and your results when you take a new assignment. What are your favorite tools for reflection? How will you build reflection into your routines? Who will ask you great questions that will get you to reflect? What questions do you need to regularly reflect on?

What Organizations Can Do

Celebrate success. Who are the women breaking barriers in your organization? Create opportunities to recognize their achievements—in their fields and in their efforts to help other women. The effect of these celebrations is critical to building a pipeline of women talent.

Incentivize role models. The quickest way to start a movement is to tap into those who have succeeded. We find that once people feel good about their progress, they are eager to help others. Use that to create a group of mentors, sponsors, and guides.

Train your managers. Are your managers giving equitable challenging assignments to all genders on their teams? Whether it's educating about inclusion or increasing the amount of challenging stretch assignments, investing in line managers is the first step toward increasing opportunities for growth.

> **Ensure internal support is available.** Sometimes women STEM employees need a sounding board and may not feel safe with their line manager or immediate circle. Ensuring that there are internal coaches or support personnel and that all leaders in the organization are aware of who their resources are can help create those developmental spaces.

CRASHING THE GOOD OLD BOYS' PARTY

Remember your first job? Meeting colleagues, learning the language, engaging your first project, first success, and even first failure? Most people have a horror story or two from their first job. Maybe it involved a bad boss, coworkers you didn't mesh with, or difficulty adjusting to new responsibilities. However, for technical women entering the workplace, the first job experience often comes with a unique set of challenges.

Men continue to dominate STEM fields, and even when women break into the workplace, they may find themselves excluded or singled out, or have their accomplishments belittled. In the wake of #MeToo and the rise of a Millennial and GenZ workforce there's less patience for hazing and exclusion. But such behavior still operates in some STEM organizations. In a time when people strive to build cultures of equity in organizations and in societies, it's necessary that we look clearly at the degree of challenge women have and continue to face in STEM fields. This chapter examines the challenges technical women face from the "good old boys" they work with and how they can be overcome.

When Beverly began her first job as a process engineer in the steel industry, she was fortunate to have a boss who was supportive and excited about having another engineer on the team, regardless of their gender. However, her boss's enthusiasm did little to spare her from hazing.

The first time Beverly went to work on-site at one customer's factory, the customer stopped her in her tracks. He asked her to wait before entering the factory, returned to his office, and called her boss to ask if it was a joke that the woman at his factory doorstep was supposed to be an engineering employee from his firm. Beverly's boss asserted that she was in fact the process engineer assigned to the customer's company and that he was confident they would work well together. While Beverly waited, the customer wasn't convinced and asked Beverly's boss to re-confirm several times that he was serious about assigning a woman engineer.

Her supportive boss could not protect Beverly from the hazing she endured while at the customer's site. As a process engineer, Beverly was responsible for final product testing in the steel rolling mill, for which she needed samples to test. Members of the rolling mill production team decided they were going to test Beverly, and they gave her big, unwieldy hunks of metal as test samples. Though it was probably dangerous for Beverly to lift those samples, she looked on the bright side—at least she was getting a workout! Beverly wrangled the pieces they gave her and completed her testing, refusing to give them any satisfaction. When the technicians finally realized that Beverly wasn't going to succumb to the hazing and that they had a serious project engineer on their hands, they stopped. Reflecting on her experience, Beverly repeats an old adage: "What doesn't kill you makes you stronger—literally," she says.

Over the years, Beverly has developed strategies and tactics for communicating and building credibility in environments dominated by men. "Scientists are always so condescending and superior," she says. "That's just how they operate. I always find a way to make sure they know my qualifications at the beginning of a meeting. It makes the meeting much more efficient if I can get acknowledgement of my role and expertise out of the way so I'm not fighting for it throughout."

Not all of us have endured the level of hazing Beverly did. Hearing her story, it's hard to imagine this level of animosity. Yet these kinds of experiences do happen, and stories like Beverly's were all too common for those early women in STEM.

Exclusion Exhaustion

The notion of the boys' club is a well-known factor in women's organizational experiences. In companies dominated by this culture, women are often excluded in networks and social environments outside of the office where decisions and deals are made. And because technical women almost always work in environments dominated by men, they face boys'-club-style exclusion on a regular basis, in almost every phase of their careers.

Examples of what women experience are plentiful in the media. In June 2019, for example, *GQ* came under fire after the magazine published a photo featuring a group of tech entrepreneurs during a trip in Italy. The only two women in the photo had been photoshopped into it after the group forgot to include them in the original photo-op.

In October 2018, physicist Donna Strickland became just the third woman out of 209 recipients to receive the Nobel Prize in physics. Strickland wasn't especially interested in the focus on gender that media took in reporting the honor. "I see myself as a scientist, not a woman in science," she said in an interview with *The Guardian*. However, Strickland's gender was hard not to note since just days prior several news publications reported on a presentation by physicist Alessandro Strumia in which he was reported to say that men invented physics and participation in it was not by invitation (Chawla, 2019). It's not hard to interpret Strumia's remarks: Women are not invited to work in the field of physics and their achievements aren't noteworthy.

The "Only Woman in the Room"

Have you ever felt alone in a room? Like you didn't quite fit in with a group? Do you ever think how tiring it must feel to not be part of the in group—to be alone while surrounded by an organization of people? It's a feeling impossible to ignore if you're the only woman in the room. Women in STEM report that the worst thing about being the only woman in the room is how exhausting it is. These women resent always having to be on guard;

they never know where the hazing will come from, what meetings or strategy sessions they will not be invited to, or when their expertise and credentials will be questioned. The constant requirement that technical women have to reiterate, explain, and rationalize their decisions gets really tiring, so much so that sometimes these women just let it slide, and let others take credit for their ideas, or worse, they decide not to offer ideas and solutions that they will have to defend. Add that to the fact that they never know when they are going to be asked to take notes or get the coffee—tasks rarely requested of men—having a relaxed, collaborative, productive meeting is a rare occurrence. One woman jokingly described the anxiety she felt in the workplace as "like being Jamie Lee Curtis in a Halloween movie, you never know when the guy in the mask with the knife will pop up."

Women in STEM generally feel supported at work and want to believe their workplace to be one of equity. It's over time and with deeper consideration that patterns of exclusion experienced in the workplace emerge. In 2015, Professionals Australia, an employee's association, released a report looking at the experiences of women in the STEM professions. In a survey of 400 women, 55 percent of respondents said that women in STEM often must prove themselves, where men are assumed to be capable.

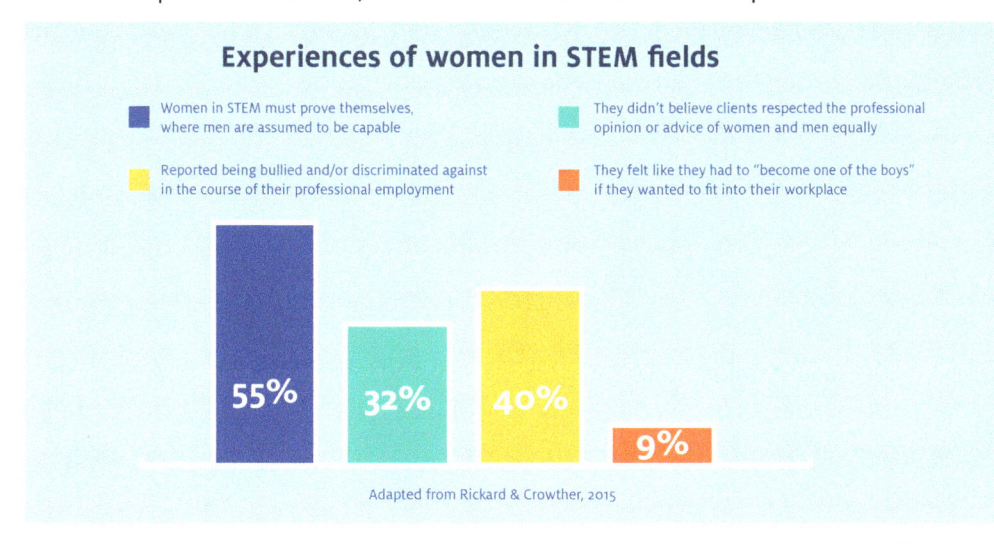

Experiences of women in STEM fields

- Women in STEM must prove themselves, where men are assumed to be capable — 55%
- Reported being bullied and/or discriminated against in the course of their professional employment — 40%
- They didn't believe clients respected the professional opinion or advice of women and men equally — 32%
- They felt like they had to "become one of the boys" if they wanted to fit into their workplace — 9%

Adapted from Rickard & Crowther, 2015

Nearly 32 percent of those surveyed said they didn't believe clients respected the professional opinion or advice of women and men equally. Approximately 40 percent reported being bullied and/or discriminated against in the course of their professional employment. And 9 percent said they felt like they had to "become one of the boys" if they wanted to fit into their workplace (Rickard & Crowther, 2015).

All too often, senior leadership in organizations downplay the effect of the boys' club culture still often inherent in STEM fields. Some try to justify excluding women by saying "it's for their own good," because if they were included, they might feel uncomfortable. Others claim it's not a big deal when women are hazed because "it's all in good fun." However, when women are excluded because of their gender, it's not only a hindrance to their professional development, but an obstacle to their company's success.

"It's Just a Joke"

Virginia knew from an early age what she wanted to be when she grew up. She wanted to help people. She was good at building things and making mechanical things work. She was fascinated with the first artificial heart and followed the compelling story of Barney Clark, Dr. Denton Cooley, and Dr. Michael DeBakey the way other kids follow comic book heroes. As she watched Clark's epic 112-day tale of survival with an artificial heart unfold, she realized her destiny: to design bio-machines. She wanted to make medical devices that could improve and save people's lives.

Virginia took all the right steps to realize her dream. She graduated top in her class in mechanical engineering from a respected university and landed the perfect engineering job at a prestigious hospital in New York City designing cutting-edge orthopedic implants. The opportunity seemed like a dream come true. As a newly minted engineer and a small-town girl, Virginia approached her first day with excitement and fear. What would it be like to finally live the dream? She found out soon enough.

Virginia was assigned to work in a computer room with four men, but when she arrived at the room, a sign on the door stopped her in her tracks. "He-Man Woman-Haters Club," the sign read. She later learned it was a reference to the clubhouse in the 1950s TV show *Little Rascals*—a place where the young boys featured in the comedy show didn't allow girls. But at that moment she knew nothing about the show, and she was stunned and hurt. She didn't know how to respond. Summoning up all her courage, she opened the door—only to be met by a group of four men laughing hilariously. Her new colleagues thought the shocked look on her face was priceless. They explained that it was "just a joke," but it certainly wasn't the welcome she was expecting.

Virginia's negative experience could have ended there, and the guys could've pulled down the sign. But it didn't. Her colleagues continued what they felt was good-natured hazing on a regular basis. They flashed suggestive pictures on her computer screen, posted postcards of bikini-clad women from their Caribbean vacations, and were never shy about using other ways to remind her that she didn't really belong in their boys' club.

Moving On

Like Beverly, Virginia didn't let the hazing get to her. She focused on her work and became noticeably accomplished in a short period of time. After a while she eventually became good friends with some of the men in her group, who genuinely seemed to think there wasn't anything wrong with their "good-natured joking."

The tables turned two years later, when Virginia was promoted to lead the group. The men she worked with said they respected that her hard work and talent earned her the recognition. None of them questioned that she was the most qualified person for the job. But they did get a surprise. As she took on her new role, she told them to take down the postcards immediately and made it clear that now the joking was over—for good.

"You Wouldn't Be Comfortable"

One way to understand bias is as explicitly excluding a group of people. Second-generation bias is somewhat less explicit. It presents itself when a culture informally excludes a group of people in the way it's constructed and supported in practices and in perspectives. In our experience, women in technical fields report that they almost always face second-generation bias at work. Sabina's story is an example of that bias in action.

Fresh out of college, Sabina joined a small company as the only woman in a non-administrative role. The company's annual planning meeting was held in Las Vegas, but she wasn't invited. When she asked her boss why she couldn't participate in the meeting, he said the "venue was not suitable for her" and went on to say that she may feel uncomfortable "with all the boys" in Las Vegas." After that incident, she left that company to look for a job where she would be included in decision making and treated fairly as a woman. Sabina says the biggest lesson she drew from her exclusion experience was that she belonged in a company culture that is inclusive and diverse or that she should take a role where she could influence and help build such a culture. Sabina believes—has always believed—she deserves a seat at the table, and she hasn't settled for less since that early experience. The only positive thing to come from it is the gratitude she feels about that negative experience occurring early in her career. That allowed her to take the lessons from it and apply them to future jobs.

It's important to realize how bias shows up and to reflect on how an individual's reaction is pivotal to leadership outcomes. Sabina demonstrated her strength and perseverance despite explicit gender bias.

"It's About Your Wedding"

After about four years at HP and a slew of wonderful managers, I (Kelly) felt compelled to take my current manager to lunch for a difficult conversation. I had been based in Mexico for nearly two years and had a good relationship with this manager. Over lunch, we exchanged pleasantries, reviewed the outcomes of the supply chain redesign effort I had led, and discussed his vision for the division. Then I brought up the difficult topic that was the reason I had called the meeting in the first place. My project had wrapped up three weeks prior, and I hadn't been assigned any new work. I wanted to know why that was. I was feeling bored and unproductive.

"Kelly," he began, "I was looking at the different project areas, and I know you are getting ready for your wedding, and mostly, I do not want to overload you." As he said these words, a giant pit formed in my stomach, I was grasping for words. How was this "nice guy" not giving me work because of my wedding? I found myself acting courteous toward his "thoughtfulness" while insisting that he assign me to a project, as I had the bandwidth for a normal workload. "Si, si, si," he assured, but I was not convinced. I remember fuming, thinking that there is no way that my fiancé's boss would have made this assumption.

The fact that my manager was always pleasant to work with made this experience especially difficult. We had hosted him for dinner, I knew his family, and I trusted him. His biased behavior came out of the fact that he truly thought he was doing me a favor. This was classic second-generation bias, but definition aside, the challenge facing me then was figuring out what to do with it. When I started my career at HP, gender bias could not have been further from my mind. Even when I noticed that most executives fell into the tall-white-male category, and even after I learned that a man who started six months after me was making more than I was within a year, I still felt that the future was full of opportunities for me. This lunch conversation with my manager changed all of that. I tried to keep the relationship positive, but my workload never met my expectations, and I lost trust with my manager. When I facilitated my first workshop for technical women 20 years later, I looked back for the moments that inspired me to take on that kind of work. That lunch encounter was one of those moments.

"Your Presence Isn't Required"

While Kelly's story describes personal and professional impact resulting from bias, Joy's story illustrates not only the personal and professional toll but the negative business impact of prolonged gender bias.

During her time leading the human factors and usability function department at her organization, Joy was responsible for establishing a new lab as part of a strategic initiative to support the company's need for products that people could use more easily. At the time, Joy's role was not a well understood discipline at the company or in the tech world in general, and the product engineering teams (consisting mostly of men) at her organization dismissed it as "soft engineering." As the only woman, Joy was regularly excluded from meetings that were integral to her job.

For Joy's team to integrate itself into the product development process at the right time, it needed regularly updated knowledge of product schedules and potential delays. Product status and challenges were discussed monthly in product director staff meetings. But even though Joy was a director, her boss believed that because she wasn't responsible for a specific product, she wouldn't be comfortable in the meeting. After each monthly meeting, her boss gave Joy a brief report. Then Joy had to schedule time-consuming individual meetings with each director and her own team to reconstruct the decisions and discussions.

Joy's exclusion from the director staff meetings created a much longer and less effective product development process. This negatively impacted her team's morale. It should have been obvious that the additional meeting and coordination time Joy's team needed could be eliminated if testing was integrated into the product development cycle. It would be easier to balance resources between the product groups if Joy were included in the product directors' meetings, rather than dealing with them after the fact. More importantly, from a strategic perspective, excluding her and her team denied Joy a platform for championing the value of usability as the company's markets expanded.

Joy suspected she wasn't being included because she was one of the very few senior engineers at the company who was a woman. She frequently confronted her boss about the inefficiency of the process. He told her repeatedly that her presence wasn't necessary and would probably be a distraction. It wasn't until her boss left the company that she was finally invited to the product directors' meetings and the other directors quickly realized what they had been missing.

Overcoming Exclusion

Joy's experience illustrates the negative impact the "boys' club mentality" can have on a company's bottom line. Diversity and inclusion mean more than hiring different kinds of people—in this case, women. It's about ensuring they feel welcome. In 2016, nonprofit organization Catalyst released a report looking at day-to-day experiences of workplace inclusion and exclusion. According to that report, researchers found that exclusion comes at a great cost to organizations in the form of compromised job satisfaction, lower sense of well-being, reduced work effort, diminished employee voice, and greater intention to leave. Conversely, the Catalyst report indicates that when employees feel included in their wor environment, organizational commitment, trust, well-being, creativity, and innovation improve (Nugent, Pollack, and Travis, 2016).

Exclusion can often be traced to underlying assumptions that themselves are rooted in gender bias. Lisa tells of the time she was presented a

Impact of exclusion on day-to-day experiences

| Compromised job satisfaction | Lower sense of well-being | Reduced work effort | Diminished employee voice | Greater intention to leave |

Conversely, the Catalyst report indicates that when employees feel included in their work environment, organizational commitment, trust, well-being, creativity, and innovation improve.

Adapted from Nugent, Pollack, and Travis, 2016

prestigious company award. It was a special opportunity as the award was normally given to teams—to be singled out as an individual was extremely rare. As she made the rounds at the banquet that preceded the award announcements, she discovered that many of the executives she met assumed it was her husband who had received the award. Actually, Lisa's husband was a stay-at-home dad. Those kinds of assumptions, she says, signal that women don't really belong among the top performers or merit the highest company accolades.

Bias All the Way Down

While working at marketing firm Regis McKenna Inc (RMI) in the 1980s, I (Patty) dealt with many tech startups in Silicon Valley. At the time, RMI had a stellar record when it came to gender diversity. However, despite the prevalence of women at the company and in the marketing industry overall, women weren't spared from the boys' club mentality of the tech clients we served. While working with Apple, the women on the team were dubbed the "Regettes" by Guy Kawasaki, and the name didn't exactly carry a positive connotation. In his 1990 book, *The Macintosh Way*, Kawasaki describes it this way:

> "'Regettes' is an affectionate and sadistic term for account executives from a famous Silicon Valley PR agency called Regis McKenna, Inc.," Kawasaki writes. "Typically, they wear Laura Ashley suits and one week after graduating from college with a BA in Fine Arts, they tell t-shirt clients how to sell their products. If you ever meet someone who has a friend at Regis McKenna, the conversation always starts like this: 'I have a friend at Regis McKenna, but she's not like the rest of them'" (p. 126).

Despite Kawasaki's assertion that *Regette* was an affectionate term, many women at Regis McKenna strongly resented it. We saw it as just one more form of the not-so-subtle hazing and exclusion we experienced. I (Patty) didn't work with the Apple team and I didn't know Guy Kawasaki, but I felt the impact of this insulting nickname. For example, when I told people where I worked, I was often asked, with a bit of a knowing chuckle, if I was one of the Regettes. Guy Kawasaki was an important figure in Silicon Valley and venture capital, and so the nickname became well known and haunted many of us for years. The higher percentage of women in marketing did not offer the women at Regis McKenna immunity from the exclusion and hazing that women in STEM experience frequently throughout their careers. But like so many women of the day, we just kind of brushed it off and moved forward.

A decade later, when I presented to VCs on the boards of the companies I worked for, or later, as consulting clients, the name would occasionally be mentioned. I often wondered who might be thinking of me as a 'Regette', unconsciously questioning my ideas and recommendations. As with many of the women we interviewed, I never knew when this bias would rear its ugly head, so I felt I had to be over-prepared and constantly prove myself. And like the women we meet in this book, most of my colleagues at Regis McKenna developed successful careers despite this sexist insult. Some of us became C- and VP level executives, some took faculty positions at top-tier universities, some started and ran important companies—some even became respected authors. I guess Guy got it wrong!

"It's Just Not a Big Deal"

A common thread running through the stories successful STEM women told us was that they often decide not to dwell on incidents of exclusion—to just get past it and move on. They often give their colleagues and customers the benefit of the doubt, saying that while the men may be aware that what they're doing is wrong, they don't think it's a big deal. The women equate bad behavior with immaturity, often referring to these exclusionary experiences as "frat-boy hazing."

But these incidents have a more lasting impact than many women admit. The memories are still poignant and crystal clear decades after they occur. The incidents seem to be particularly painful early in their careers, when they are in new jobs and feeling vulnerable, when they haven't yet developed the confidence and thick skin that comes later. Though successful technical women get past it and move on, these experiences do impact their ability to just get their work done and be valuable contributors to their teams. As Beverly says, "We just want to be a full functioning member of the team and you often can't be—you don't get really integrated into the team the way men do"

Few exclusion experiences can match the story Magdalena Yesil tells in her 2017 book, *Power Up: How Smart Women Win in the New Economy*. A pioneering engineer in Silicon Valley, Magdalena worked at Advanced Micro Devices in the 1980s. She was invited to the national sales conference in Las Vegas to present information on the new product she had helped develop. Her presentation was on the first day of the conference, which began with what the agenda called an "eye-opener." Magdalena's eyes were opened all right—the curtains drew back to reveal topless women in a dance routine. Of course, that kind of company presentation would be illegal today, but it's amazing that this type of thing could happen just 30 years ago.

Like many of the women we spoke with, Magdalena took control of the situation, vowing she would never feel so powerless again. She confronted the CEO Jerry Saunders and was invited to join his group for dinner where she made her disgust and disappointment abundantly clear. Such shows were banned from future conferences, and Magdalena gained respect for taking a stand. Though she didn't succeed in completely changing what she calls the "patriarchy culture" at AMD, she did put a few dents in it and took the first step in what she calls the "power of self-advocacy" so critical to her own success. Magdalena went on to become a Silicon Valley venture capitalist, the first investor in Salesforce, and one of its founding board members.

Boys Will be Boys?

The focus of this chapter has been on the bias and exclusionary practices inherent in the good old boys' club. But our colleague Mary reminds us that gender biases can themselves be gender free. "When I was in my first engineering role, I was the youngest of the group and the only woman," Mary says. "The mail carrier came by one day pushing her cart, looking for our group's admin. I was sitting with my male colleagues in a design discussion for a new integrated circuit chip and the mail carrier saw me, walked into the room and handed me the mail, assuming I was the admin. And you guessed it, she was a woman. I was mortified and embarrassed and she thought nothing of it since in her world, I couldn't possibly be one of the engineers!" Perhaps such an assumption would be rarer today, but we can't presume that the bias that affects women in STEM presents itself only in men. Especially second-generation bias, which is embedded so deeply in cultural structures that it's the "normal" way to think.

Successful women in STEM recognize, at some point in their careers, that the key to thriving in fields dominated by men often has less to do with crashing the boys' club party and more to do with turning adversaries into advocates. As Virginia puts it, "Converting adversaries to allies does not require a long time but it does require establishing mutual understanding, respect, trust, demonstrating your contribution, and yes, some hard work and patience. Not too much patience," she notes, "but enough to give working relationships time to build." Above all, Virginia reminds us, women should cultivate a determination to meet commitments that advance the organization's business strategy. We discuss how successful technical women rise because they develop business acumen in chapter four and the development of allies in chapter five.

The Identity of Persistence

A woman working in a technical field is almost always the only woman in the room throughout her entire career. She is probably one of a handful of women in a graduating class and that ratio usually doesn't change as she enters the job force. This aloneness and feeling of otherness contribute to the high quit rate for technical women. Forty-five percent of women leave STEM fields after beginning their careers there (Williams, 2018).

Given that many women who stay in STEM and build successful careers move on from exclusionary incidents suggests something in play other than a generous personality or a thick skin. And in fact, some research points to a mitigating factor that can in some women lessen the impact of gender bias:

the combination of a strong sense of gender identity and a strong sense of STEM identity. In a study by Cathleen Clerkin, women in STEM were asked whether they see their gender and STEM identities as integrated or separate, and their intention to remain or leave their career in the next few years. Clerkin's study suggests that women who see their gender identity and professional STEM identity as a combined identity (rather than two competing or conflicted identities) are more likely to stay in their chosen STEM field than those who don't (2019). In other words, while it may be that technical women can move on from bias and exclusionary encounters, if they are grounded in their identity as a woman in STEM, their ability to move on is strengthened. It pays to hang on to that geek girl inside.

> **Women who see their gender identity and professional STEM identity as a combined identity...are more likely to stay in their chosen STEM field.**

Takeaways, Tips, and Tools

- The 'good old boys' culture remains a challenge and is magnified for women in STEM fields. Since technical women are always in environments dominated by men from high school through retirement, they face exclusion on a regular basis, in almost every facet of their careers. Discrimination cannot be tolerated at the organizational level, and it is incumbent upon organizational leaders to enact policies that demand zero tolerance and provide education for all employees on what behaviors are accepted and which are not.

- Women rarely blame the men who excluded them. They more often simply move on and, except in the most egregious situations, use it as an opportunity to educate the men who have excluded them. In some cases, they even establish bonds with these men over time and form alliances.

- Women who persist and hold the line in their careers despite bias and discrimination share consistent characteristics. One is a clear sense of both gender and professional identity. Women who persevere show that rather than letting hazing keep them from achieving their goals, it motivates them to push themselves harder, turning anger and embarrassment into fuel for being the best.

What You Can Do

All of us have some of the protective wear needed for dealing with gender bias. Tapping into your own sense of self and connection with your profession can help carry you through the storms that these encounters with the good old boys may produce. Think about how the following ideas (and similar ones you come up with) can help you recognize bias and fight exclusion.

> **Battle unconscious bias at work.** Everyone has biases. Even women in STEM. The key is to acknowledge them. Paying attention to the positive traits in colleagues who are different from you builds your "diversity quotient." It takes strength and awareness to work across differences.

> **Flip your script.** One of the best ways to break your own bias is to notice a habit and practice breaking it. Lean into yes, when you normally say no. Work with people of differently identified genders to confront the stereotypes you automatically assume of others—the more you expose yourself to diversity, the weaker the stereotype becomes. Seek commonalities over difference. Commit to expressing as little sexism as

possible in your interactions. That's the easy part. The hard part is to act on your commitments. Learn how you can best become a public ally for social justice related to gender. Be willing to upset the status quo.

Retrain your brain. Start with your own innate biases. Here are some examples: She's too nice; she wouldn't want this job. She has young children; the travel schedule will be too demanding. He won't want this role; it's too much like what he is doing now. How can you explore your assumptions and take action to defuse or shift them? Follow this process:

1. Identify an assumption you hold that you have determined is a bias.

2. Is it true? How do you absolutely know?

3. What is the payoff of having this belief?

4. What are the costs of having this belief?

5. Who would you be without that thought/belief?

6. Reframe the thought to a different message. Is the new message as true as or truer than the original one?

Build bias immunity. In the face of bias and exclusion, leaving an unhealthy work environment is a valid option in some but not all cases. More important is how you make the best choice for yourself and keep your focus tuned and resources at the ready. While no one should expect a woman to have to develop a thick skin simply to do her best work, developing a robust resilience to deal with bias and exclusion is a must. Resilience also plays a broader role, fortifying you to handle the inevitable setbacks you are likely to encounter in your career.

Reach out for support. The boys' club is a social network. Do you have your own social network? Talking through challenges with colleagues helps generate novel approaches, and support from trusted allies can alleviate the stress of challenging situations. The best antidote to the boys' club? Your club.

Connect with your sense of purpose. Connecting to some larger mission beyond your own success will help you face life's struggles. Remind yourself of your personal "why" every day. See chapter one for ways you can practice.

Give yourself credit. You have the resources within you to be more resilient. Set aside 15 minutes and make a list of times in your personal life or professional life where you struggled, survived, and bounced back. What did you do? What did you learn? Draw on these skills and insights.

Stop ruminating. Where is your mind right now? Is it replaying the past or dwelling anxiously on the future? Such rumination causes the brain to produce cortisol and you to experience stress. Interrupt your brain's unhealthy rumination habit and focus on your experience of the present moment. Learn mindfulness or focusing techniques to train your brain to stop creating its own stress (Roger & Petrie, 2017).

Embrace learning. Do you find yourself facing a recurring situation but unable to adopt a new approach? Maybe it is time to try something new. Make learning a habit and try to learn something new each day. Notice when you are open to learning and when you resist it. Find a trusted learning partner who can give you objective feedback and support.

Take care of yourself. Sleep more, eat better, and exercise. Good physical health goes a long way toward boosting your mental and emotional health. Leave an unhealthy work environment if necessary and feasible. Most importantly, make the best choices for yourself by aligning your values with your work and your career plans.

What Organizations Can Do

Build inclusion into talent conversations. Informal and formal talent conversations can house unconscious bias. Some simple practices foster a culture of equitable and inclusive development by encouraging leaders to see the whole person across from them during reviews. For example, ask each leader in your organization to respond to the following question: Who are you mentoring? Who are you sponsoring?

Don't make men the normal choice for promotion and career advancements. Look hard at past practices. Was there a time when several candidates were being considered for a role and they were all men, perhaps all white men? If so, how did that come to be? If mostly white men applied for the opening, consider whether the position description or something about hiring practices discouraged others.

Recognize talent hidden by bias. Ensure that the measures used to gauge success at your organization are objective. For example, have HR review and further vet talent recommendations by managers across a rubric of objective measures to ensure more inclusive retention and promotion. Think about what should and should not play into how talent is evaluated. Prepare a plan to deal with unconscious bias as you advocate for more diverse talent.

BRINGING A BUSINESS PERSPECTIVE

If you want to be in a better position—with a job you like more with better pay, with better long-term opportunities, and with greater security—you need to understand the key drivers of the business and use that knowledge to make a contribution, according to Kevin Cope. "If you want to be a more effective leader, you need to be better able to engage your team and link your team's actions with the overall needs and strategic goals of the company," he says. Cope consults with organizations on how to instill business acumen and fiscal responsibility in employees in non-finance roles.

Cope observes in his work with hundreds of companies that engineers and technical teams often show the least appreciation of the value of business acumen. "Even though they are numbers-savvy and have a better aptitude for finance than most people, they often have a bit of arrogance about being concerned about profits," he says. "There's a prevailing attitude that finance is up to the bean counters, not to the engineers. I've heard engineers say, "Leave it to the bean-counters, that's not my job." In one humorous, if telling story, Cope shares a conversation in which he reassured a senior manager at NASA that business acumen isn't rocket science. The engineer replied, "I wish it were, then I could understand it!" (K Cope, personal communication, September 11, 2019).

Our readers might ask why we're starting this chapter about women and business perspective using a perspective from a man. And what does gender have to do with it, anyway? As it turns out, gender plays a critical role in how women are prepared for senior positions in technical companies. Susan Colantuono (2016), CEO of Leading Women, discovered two critical factors in her research about advancing women to executive levels of organizations. The first factor sounds logical: Individuals seen as high potentials use their skills, talents, and abilities to help organizations achieve strategic and financial goals by working well with others inside and outside of the organization. But when it comes to moving up in an organization, business and financial acumen are twice as important as engaging well with others.

The second important point highlighted in her research (and the reason we wrote this chapter) is that almost all the men she interviewed, but virtually none of the women, were told about the importance of meeting strategic and financial goals as they moved up in their careers. Men receive clear communication that business and financial acumen are critically important to advance into senior leadership roles but very few women are given that same message. Instead, women more often hear that they need to develop more skill in such areas as engaging well with others, communication, and self-promotion (Colantuono, 2016).

CCL's review of the critical leadership challenges of thousands of leaders over the past decade reinforces Colantuono's findings. Mid-level leaders seeking to advance to executive levels of leadership overwhelmingly identify their main challenge as business strategy and change. People development and communication are further down the list.

It's heartening to see that many technical women have figured this out on their own. The passion that women in STEM have for solving complex problems often gets channeled to business problems as they advance in their careers. These women develop business acumen with a focus on how technology can accelerate business goals. They are often promoted over technical men because of this strategic view. In this chapter, we look at how making a business perspective part of technical know-how becomes an important strategy in the advancement of technical women. It's an important path toward promotion and recognition, and it becomes ever more critical as women ascend the career ladder, where the ranks of senior leaders become increasingly filled with men.

Business Acumen: The Route to the C-Suite

An investment in business education eased the track to the executive suite for many of the women leaders we interviewed. Sumitha, a vice president in a Cloud SaaS company providing tech solutions for the transportation and logistics industry, was a successful engineering manager on a fast promotion track but felt she wanted to and could do something more personally satisfying. She reflected on her career as she was planning maternity leave for the birth of her second child. "I was having thoughts about moving into a tech leadership position," she says. "I felt I was a good manager, but not really a true leader. I was looking for personal growth—professional, spiritual, intellectual. Getting a broader business perspective seemed like the right next step."

> **I realized the importance of understanding how what my engineering team is working on connects with the broader goals of the company and with what's going on in the industry.**

Sumitha spent three years earning her MBA from the Haas School of Management at UC Berkeley—while performing her job as an engineering manager. "I dove right in," she says. "My son was born during spring break!" Sumitha describes the two years of very intense learning covering all aspects of business and leadership as eye opening and a critical shift in perspective. "I realized the importance of understanding how what my engineering team is working on connects with the broader goals of the company and with what's going on in the industry. Now I'm always looking for ways to connect top down and bottom up. Top down to see what the missing links are between strategy and execution and bottom up to ensure that everything we do aligns with the broader company strategy and industry trends," she says.

Sumitha realized how an engineering mindset has to evolve in order for women in technical fields to become effective business leaders. "As engineers, we like the pure logic of programming. It either works or it doesn't. It's either black or white. There is no guesswork," she says. "Even if the problem is complex, you know you can solve it if you stick with it and you'll be rewarded with an answer. But business problems are different and don't always have clear answers. It's very challenging for engineers to tie technology successes into business goals."

Many technical women have found that taking online or community college finance and business courses can give them the fundamentals they need to understand and monitor business and market trends in addition to technology advances. In its work, CCL recommends that the companies it works with include business acumen and negotiation as a regular part of their women's leadership programs. And CCL takes its own medicine. It strongly encourages its employees to participate in a two-day business acumen course. The learning pays off as team members at all levels learn to understand a customer's business and how its leadership development recommendations contribute to their business strategies.

Growth Mindset and Business Perspective

In order to include a business and strategic perspective in your development toward a leadership role, you need not just the capacity to know more, but to learn deeper and to incorporate new concepts into familiar activities. Carol Dweck has labeled this capacity *a growth mindset*. As compared with *a fixed mindset*, in which intelligence and knowledge is

> **But to get to senior director and VP, you have to prove that your teams and decisions are supporting the business goal,"** she says. **"You have to have business sense or you won't make it.**

thought of as static and innate, a growth mindset accommodates continuous learning (2006).

CCL talks about this perspective as *learning agility*—more than learning new skills, it's about continually applying skills to different experiences. It also refers to giving up skills that no longer work in present circumstances and leaving behind perspectives and ideas that are no longer relevant to learn new ones that are applicable (Hallenbeck, 2016). As Sumitha notes, in STEM fields there is usually one "right answer" and a solution to a problem. Expanding one's mindset is key to helping broaden perspectives and tolerate ambiguity when there is not always one right answer—as in the world of business. Technical leaders we interviewed showed how to apply their technical problem-solving skills to that different world. Taking the initiative to develop a business perspective is helping women in STEM reframe the way they prioritize, organize, and communicate the work they do. As Marshall Goldsmith aptly put it, "What got you here won't get you to where you want to go" (2014). People are promoted because they stand out, not because they fit in. Tying business acumen to technical expertise is a standout strategy.

Bringing a business perspective is a process of helping the organization think not just about its technology or science but about how it can use technology to deliver on its strategy and financial targets. And it's dependent on the fact that the work itself is often a deep source of learning. As we discussed in chapter two, the right on-the-job developmental experiences produce lessons that carry forward into a career.

Customer Obsessed

At Amazon, Jeff Bezos sets up an empty chair at each meeting to be the chair of the customer. What would the customer say about our current conversation? What is the customer needing now and how are we addressing it? The chair is an ever-present reminder in the meeting that business perspective and customer perspective go hand in hand (Thompson, 2016).

Let's come back to Sumitha's story. While earning her MBA, she was recruited into a director of technical marketing position reporting to the chief marketing officer. Her stint in marketing was invaluable, and she was able to apply many of the concepts from her MBA. "It stretched my muscles in so many ways. I learned so much from direct customer exposure. And I finally got over my imposter syndrome that was so self-limiting," she says. *Imposter syndrome* can be defined as the paranoid, debilitating suspicion that you are a fraud—crippling otherwise high-achieving people (women and men) so that they "don't feel like they deserve their accomplishments and that they have faked their way to success" (Martineau & Mount, 2019, p. 91).

Sumitha sees more people moving out of pure engineering to hybrid roles that are user-facing, using technology to solve user problems. But she has also experienced backlash and was surprised at the emotional response from her engineering colleagues. "They considered me a 'traitor' for the move to marketing," she says. "They felt I was no longer really technical!" Sumitha went on to an operations role, focusing every day on customer experience.

It's often a leader's role to elevate the perspective of her team so that its members can develop a more critical eye toward the business and its customers. Take the case of Chris, who held chief technology officer, vice president engineering, and vice president operations positions at several fast-growing Silicon Valley startups as well as with large multinational companies. She tells a story about when she had to convince her team that customer satisfaction is always the top priority, even if it means delaying the use of the latest technology.

At the time, Chris worked in a communications company that was ready to roll out the implementation of new equipment based on exciting, cutting-edge technologies. Her team was particularly proud because many of the technologies were somewhat experimental and they would be the first to implement them in a live network. Only Chris realized that it was premature to introduce the product, since many of their customers wouldn't know how to use it. She stopped the implementation plan, even though her actions threatened to make a major impact on revenue projections. The team and other engineering managers expressed their anger that their pet technologies had been put on hold. But Chris had the backing of management, which also saw the potential disaster that the untested, untrained technology could produce. The company simply could not risk the customer dissatisfaction that could result from the product's premature release—a risk that could have produced a negative reaction that would eclipse any hoped-for customer retention and revenue.

In Chris's opinion, women can survive as engineers at the director level and below with a technology-focused view of the world. "But to get to senior director and VP, you have to prove that your teams and decisions are supporting the business goal," she says. "You have to have business sense or you won't make it."

Be the API Between Business and Technical

As Chris moved up in the management hierarchy at her organization, she herself was tagged with the reputation of not being technical enough and over time she grew hypersensitive to the fact that she didn't have deep technical skills. That changed the day the CEO told her this: "Every company needs someone who is the API between the business and the technical. That's really hard to find, and not often valued in Silicon Valley. But your ability to be that API has made a huge difference in the success of our company." Chris remembers that pivotal moment and how it shifted the way she thought about her work and her experience.

> "Every company needs someone who is the API between the business and the technical. That's really hard to find, and not often valued in Silicon Valley. But your ability to be that API has made a huge difference in the success of our company."

As engineers and scientists move up in their organizations, there is a point at which they focus more on people and general management than on science and technology. In the past, there were two distinct tracks for high-level individual contributors vs. general managers. Today's organizations often offer the possibility to move between the two. However, the move into general management and away from technology can be uncomfortable, especially for women.

For example, consider when a woman is asked to move out of a strong individual contributor role and lead a team of men because of her strong collaboration skills. If this isn't what she wants, it can pose a challenge. We often see something different: Women create a broader leadership role for themselves when they can be perceived as able to bridge the business and technical divide better than men. In other words, they become the means by which different company functions communicate and work together.

It's like the concept of the API (Application Program Interface) that Chris' boss praised her for—the method for communicating between a system's software and hardware components. Organizations might know it as a systems perspective, which is critical to their successful operation. Taking a systems perspective means identifying and considering the parts of the system and making decisions based on the amount of improvement to the system as a whole, not just to the individual parts or units. In the highly fluid business environment many organizations operate in, a systems perspective can lead to sustainable solutions to the wicked problems organizations face. Engineers have studied systems quite closely yet they can get limited in their perspective when on the job. Holding a business and technical focus requires an ability to see the whole and the parts.

I (Patty) recently mentored a high-potential engineer who was struggling with being perceived as "not technical enough." Jill is an engineering director at a software company that employs hundreds of engineers and is concerned about hiring, retaining, and promoting technical women. She had been promoted into engineering management early in her career, so she lacked the depth of working-engineer experience she might have otherwise built. Although she was a solid engineering manager and her team was meeting its milestones, she felt the team didn't respect her because of her lack of experience and technical knowledge. During the mentoring process, Jill refocused her energy to become an expert on the company's business, competition, and industry trends, and to direct the conversation to that bigger picture when she felt her technical chops were being challenged. She is now considered a thought leader within the company on the competitive and market environment and works with her teams to understand how the products they build will help the company compete, giving them a much greater appreciation of their role and impact on the company.

Fake It 'Til You Make It—And Get That Annual Report!

Sheila is the program director for next-generation robotics for a multinational mining, metals, and petroleum company—an industry extremely dominated by men. She has been with the same company for almost her entire career, starting as a researcher almost 20 years ago. Sheila embraces "not being technical enough" and believes that engineering managers can be too focused on technology knowledge. "In organizations where science and technology are a backdrop to most decisions, you have to be comfortable not being knowledgeable in all technical areas," she says. "I can't pretend to understand everything from materials science to robotics. Accepting that you don't have to know it all is key to your transition from being a technical leader to leading a P&L."

Sheila's company is focused on promoting technical women and she serves as a mentor to both men and women from STEM backgrounds at they move into management roles. "Technical people get good at data and detail, but eventually they have to manage people and work with their teams to translate technical detail into strategy and outcomes. This is a challenge for everyone with technical and scientific backgrounds, not just women. But men are more confident and seem to make that step more naturally—if they don't know it all they just push on. Women feel like they have to tick all the boxes."

Sheila finds that it's more difficult to get women than men interested in the financials. "Technical women are not as comfortable with the financials, although that's changing. I tell women, 'grab the annual report, read the financials, understand the business.' Until you do, you will never get considered for promotion because you're not broad enough. I don't care if you're uncomfortable—fake it 'til you make it."

Role Models Are Hard to Find

For early-career women in STEM, the road to the top can seem long and mysterious. Examples of women in executive roles in technical areas are few and far between. In January of 2017, the first cohort of CCL's *Advancing Technical Women* leadership journey was inaugurated in Silicon Valley. After spending a day and a half together, we looked ahead to the next three months. During that time, each woman in the program was to interview another woman in her company who was a senior business leader to learn more about her career progression and impact on the company's business.

When the assignment was announced, the room fell silent. Glancing around the room, we saw participants looking at each other, some with excitement, but others visibly struggling. At one table, three participants who work at the same corporation teamed up to see if they could get a seat at the table with the CFO of a Fortune 50 company. Another woman sent a meeting invite to her SVP by her phone right then and there.

But we also heard from one woman who said that finding a senior woman at her company was like finding a needle in a haystack. I (Patty) had heard this same challenge before in a different context. It was with a vice president of human resources at a European-based global transportation and distribution company. We were talking about ways he could increase the percentage of women in senior roles, and he cited their lack of a business perspective as the biggest barrier. "I can't promote them because they don't have a business view, they haven't been in operational roles or had P&L experience, and many don't want to take on those roles in their management rotations. I don't know why they fear it," he said.

I was reminded of the fact that at one time I believed the "women can't do math" myth and dropped my technical career aspirations because of it.

But I eventually overcame the fear of an operations role. As I moved into senior marketing positions at several Silicon Valley companies, I found I had no problem managing multimillion-dollar budgets and revenue campaigns, understanding and developing market sizing models and revenue projections, and owning the responsibility for a P&L. In fact, I was a key participant in two NASDAQ IPOs, frequently presenting to and meeting with Wall Street analysts. Not bad for a woman "who can't do math."

Drive for Efficiency, From a People Perspective

Sabina is vice president of operations at a successful fintech company responsible for building platforms for financial transactions. She jokingly describes herself as OCD—she loves order, cleanliness, and efficiency. Figuring out how to be even more efficient is almost a game for her. Driving for increased productivity, economies of scale—and thus impacting the bottom line—is her way of supporting the company's business objectives. "I come at it from a people perspective. How can I combine people, process, and tools to develop and build products more efficiently? How can I do more with less?" she asks. "My head is always full of ideas about how to do things better—I'm always looking for a new approach. I don't want to repeat what others have done, so I'm constantly selling my ideas. But I find that women have to justify their ideas more than men and that people are looking for ways to poke holes. I always come in with the 'why', the ROI, the cost reduction. I have learned to be overprepared and ready to respond to almost any question or objection. After a few meetings, you can usually establish your credibility."

Know Your S***

In recent work with a biotech start-up, we asked a woman on the executive team what she thought was needed in senior leadership. "The number one thing," she stated with no hesitation, "is that they know their s***. All the people stuff is good, but only if they know their s***."

In June's case, (we first introduced her in chapter one) her first leadership role was in a startup. She reported to a director who recognized she had people skills and was a good team leader. Even though she had the skills to stay on a technical career path, she chose to take a management path. She learned that the best way to build the team's confidence was to go deep and really understand all of the relevant data, not just the technology. "You have to know your s***", says June, "whether its technologies, marketing, finance, you have to master it. This builds everyone's confidence and there is no debate about your leadership. Women have to prove more." In other words, technical women need to be overprepared in every area. They won't move up to senior ranks on soft skills and technical expertise alone.

> "Whether its technologies, marketing, finance, you have to master it. This builds everyone's confidence and there is no debate about your leadership. Women have to prove more."

June later moved to a position as an engineering director in the software group of a Fortune 100 multinational conglomerate. When the chief technology officer of her division took a six-month leave, she had several opportunities to present to the CEO. June says, "He said he was impressed with my technical abilities, but even more impressed with my ability to translate technical concepts to business results and delivering business outcomes." Later, June was promoted to vice president based on her demonstrated ability to deliver results and in driving a major digital transformation intiative in concert with several stakeholders.

Bring a Business Perspective to Make a Difference

When any of us elevate or broaden our perspective, we are forever changed. The original goal may have been promotion. But once we have achieved that, the places we go may shift. That was certainly the case for Francesca, now the chief digital officer for a European pharmaceutical company.

Francesca realized early on the value a business perspective could bring to her career. After university, she managed clinical trials for protease inhibitors for HIV/AIDS. When she saw how these drugs completely turned around the outlook for patients from a death sentence to an almost normal life, she decided she wanted to help get such lifesaving drugs into patients' hands faster. Francesca went from the drug development bench as a PhD candidate in pharmacology to private equity and eventually to the corporate venture capital world, where she and her team provided the funding for startups developing lifesaving drugs, medical systems, and devices so that those companies could get their products into the market faster.

"I have been successful in championing these startups because I can speak science and business both," Francesca says. "My PhD gave me the scientific credibility, but I also understand how the industry works and how the drug or the technology would fit in the marketplace. I learned how to evaluate new products that merit investment funding and can really have an impact on patients' lives." Francesca shifted her mindset to catapult her work and leadership into places she had not anticipated when she was starting her career.

Takeaways, Tips, and Tools

- Technical women can leverage their strong technical and systems thinking skills and apply them to strategic business concerns.

- Technical leaders may over-focus on solving a complex problem. But often business problems don't have a single right answer.

- Maintaining a growth mindset enables technical women to become the connection between the technical and the strategic sides of the business, which broadens their leadership capacity.

Take the following lists as idea starters. Think about how they (and similar ideas you come up with, perhaps in conversation with a supportive peer, boss, or mentor) can help you broaden your perspective from technical issues to business issues such as competitive marketing and understanding a profit/loss statement. And for people charged with developing women in STEM careers, use these lists to create assignments with enough challenge and support, and think of how they might be used in a system-wide developmental strategy.

What You Can Do

Broaden your network. Make sure you are spending time with colleagues from different departments. Ask them about their business and their view of customers. Leaders often spend more time on their current network rather than thinking about their future network (Cullen, Palus, & Appaneal, 2014). Does your network need more business leaders to support your goal to broaden your perspective? Seek a mentor who is different from you in terms of knowledge and business experience.

Spend time with your customers. You probably connect with customers when you have a problem to solve. Take it a step further. Connect with them about their business problems and learn more about their organizations.

Get down to cases. Make sure you have a business case when you seek resources for a new direction, technical product, or service. How does what you need impact the business? Consider people and financials the priorities.

Expand your alerts and reading list beyond the technical. Read *The Wall Street Journal*, *Harvard Business Review*, *Strategy and Business*. Our trick: Watch CNBC or Bloomberg when you're getting ready in the morning. The day's business news can set you up for business discussions throughout the day and for learning experiences you might otherwise miss.

Articulate your company's business strategy. In *The Strategy-Focused Organization*, Robert Kaplan and David Norton (2019) bring attention to the need for every employee to understand and contribute to the company's goals. Their Balanced Scorecard has become not just a measurement tool but a means of putting strategy at the center of a company's key management processes and systems.

Cultivate your strategic brand. In CCL's Advancing Technical Women program, we suggest that women articulate a personal brand pitch directly related to the company's business strategy. How does your part of the business or the technologies you are developing connect to the strategy? To the customer's needs? Create a short pitch that you could give the CEO in an elevator that would entice them to take a meeting with you. When leaders see how your passion and focus aligns with the corporate strategy, they have an easier time promoting you into key roles.

What Your Organization Can Do

Offer and incentivize development of business acumen. Whether it's an MBA or online financial acumen course, update technical training requirements to include business acumen. Offer managers the tools to steer their technical teams to business focused conversations as part of team meetings.

Ask the CFO and their team to provide group workshops. Topics can include an overview of the company's annual report and business strategies. The people who attend can talk about how the group they are part of contributes to the business goals, through revenue production or cost savings.

Ensure inclusion in cross-functional task force teams. Embed a multi-disciplinary task force to address tough topics from a systems perspective, connecting business needs and technology needs.

THE BUDDY SYSTEM: ALLIES AND MENTORS

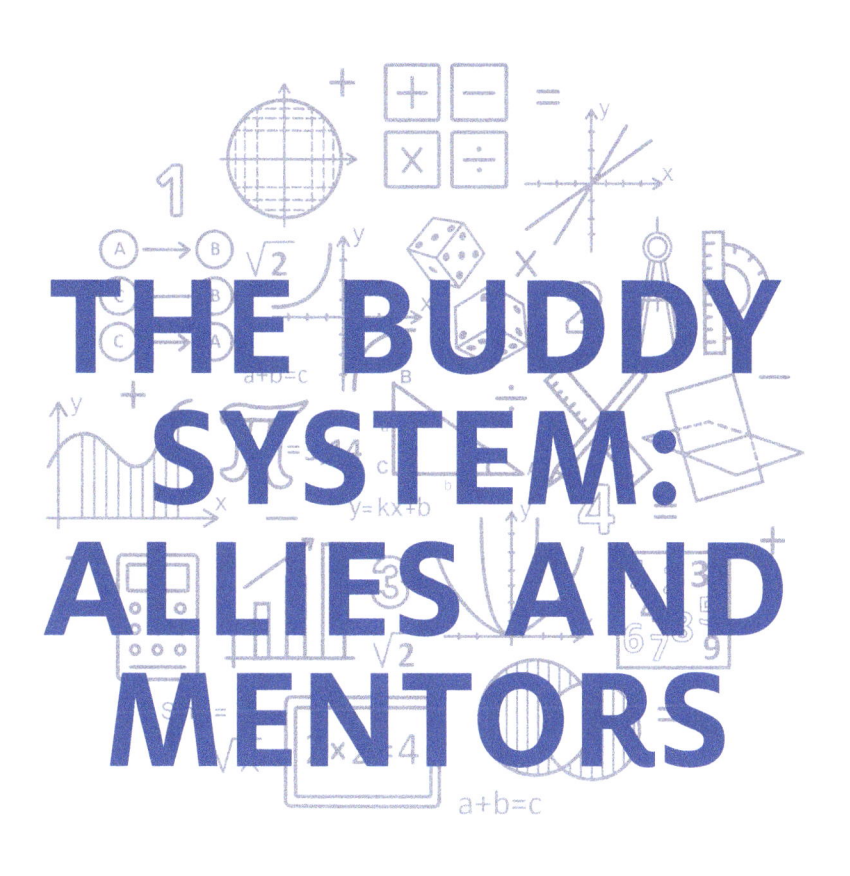

Recently, while facilitating a leadership development workshop for a group of manufacturing leaders, I (Kelly) shared my first day of work story. After graduating with my degree in mechanical engineering and taking a job with Hewlett-Packard (HP), my manager greeted me with some of the most valuable words I have ever received. "I'm going to let you make mistakes," he said. As I shared these words with those in the classroom, I could see their eyes grow wide with surprise. "Your boss said that to you on the first day of work?" someone exclaimed. And I continued sharing what he told me. "You have to have failures to learn. I won't let you make massive mistakes, but you will have space to make mistakes." This statement, contrary to what many people hear from their managers, liberated me to be fearless and try new things in my new profession.

At the time, I wasn't aware that my manager's words would be the cornerstone of my growth in innovation and leadership for years to come. My HP manager soon introduced me to my mentor, who stuck with me through my first year on the job, showing me the ropes at HP and helping me navigate the ins and outs of our workplace. In the mid-90s HP was *the* place to work for a newly minted engineer, and the knowledge and experience I gained from my supervisors and mentors there set me up for life.

My having an advocate and a mentor at the beginning of my career promoted risk taking, which in turn accelerated my development as a productive HP contributor. In this chapter we focus on the role that others play in advancing your career, and why they are even more significant for women in STEM.

Accelerating Early Career Impact

Early in her career, Patty also had mentors that gave her career-changing advice. As an account manager at PR giant Regis McKenna in the late 1980s, she was responsible for presenting the results of a customer and influencer audit to the executive team of one of her company's high-profile tech clients. As she reviewed the presentation draft with her manager, she was stopped cold when her boss saw ten bullet items on the first slide: The Executive Summary. Chris, her manager, mentor, and friend, was gentle but firm. "You call that a summary?" she said. "Our job is to distill and interpret the information for the client, not regurgitate everything we heard."

"Clients want to know the three most important things," Chris went on. "That's really about all they can take action on. It's our job to think through what's most important and to present a well-reasoned rationale for our recommendations." Finally, Chris offered this caveat: "The higher in the organization you go, the more concise you must be." Years later, Patty still remembers this advice—not just for presentations but also for simple communications like email. She keeps a quote from Thomas Jefferson posted in her office: "The most valuable of all talents is that of never using two words when one will do."

Another of Patty's mentors—Bob Metcalfe, who, along with David Boggs, invented and developed Ethernet technology—reinforced the value of precision in interacting with senior executives. "Always have an agenda with general timing for each point and stick to it," he told Patty. "Time is money, so let's not waste it." Bob was an early advocate for women in Silicon Valley and advised Patty to keep her maiden name after she married. She didn't take his advice, but she understands his reasoning: Many technical women have already established a certain level of credibility prior to marriage, and when they change their names—at least at that time—they risk erasing their hard won identities.

Most of the women we talked to for this book had mentors who helped them throughout their careers. Some of these mentors were men and others were women, but that's not as important as the clear fact that women excel in technical fields (and in other fields as well) when they have support and guidance from their peers and supervisors.

Mentoring Matters When It's Done Right

The benefits of mentoring are well-documented. Talent-development company Everwise released a report in 2018 that looked at why mentoring matters. In conducting the report, Everwise surveyed women who were receiving mentoring at their jobs. One hundred percent of them said they felt more prepared to navigate their careers in tech after participating in a mentoring program. Additionally, 82 percent said they felt they are making significant progress toward their goals (Williams, Heidi, et al., 2018).

Despite such enthusiasm and positive attitudes as expressed in the Everwise survey, many employees report dissatisfaction with the way their company executes mentoring programs. In 2008, the Clayman Institute for Gender Research released a report looking at obstacles and solutions facing mid-level women in technology. The institute surveyed 1,795 technical individuals in Silicon Valley. According to the report, 67 percent of women, compared

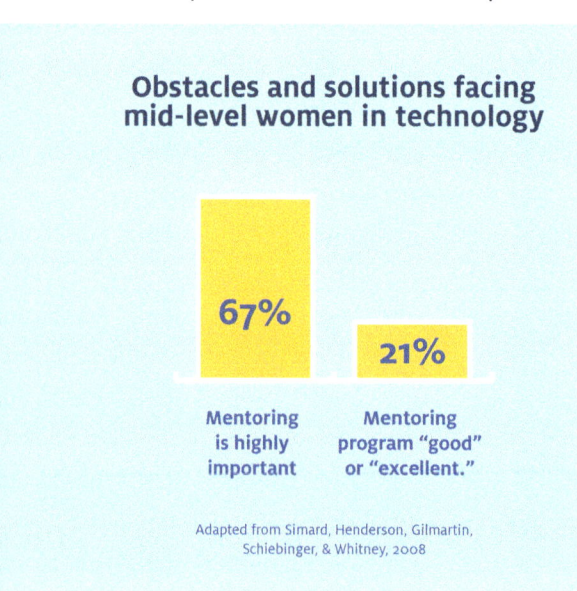

Obstacles and solutions facing mid-level women in technology

- 67% Mentoring is highly important
- 21% Mentoring program "good" or "excellent."

Adapted from Simard, Henderson, Gilmartin, Schiebinger, & Whitney, 2008 with 52 percent of men, believe mentoring is highly important. However, only 21 percent of women and 20 percent of men believe the mentoring program at their company is "good" or "excellent" (Simard, Henderson, Gilmartin, Schiebinger, & Whitney, 2008).

In order to really benefit, women in tech (this goes for men, too, and for fields outside of tech), mentoring programs must make a difference. But how do mentoring programs pull that off? One key piece: mentors should help the women they work with see and assess opportunities and threats. That means helping technical women explore the pros and cons of working on a particular project or pursuing a new opportunity. Another key to successful mentoring programs is that mentors serve as confidants, sounding boards, and personal advisors. They should transfer their knowledge, teach skills, and share their experiences. Mentors should be keenly aware of their own behavior, because the women they advise will likely follow their lead. And, finally, it's important that mentors support, validate, and encourage the women they advise.

One of the toughest things about creating a mentoring program that makes a difference is that while it is technically a simple set of tasks (coaching, listening, sharing, and so on), mentors need to execute those tasks at a high level. And that's not easy without preparation. Organizations with effective mentoring programs make sure that mentors are trained and that they are willing to devote the time required to make an impact. It's hard to find mentors for women (or for anyone else, for that matter) in companies without established programs or without people with the skills and leadership to drive such initiatives. Those gaps and absences are common to the experiences of many women in STEM, including some of those we interviewed.

Mentor Investments

Even well-planned mentoring programs fall short when mentors aren't willing to invest the time and expertise to make an impact. But successful mentoring programs can become nearly self-sustaining. Sheila is a great example of what we mean. She benefitted from a dedicated mentor early in her career and now tries to pay it forward as a mentor to other women. "I was lucky to have a woman manager who was really formative for my career," Sheila says. "She was very inspirational and a real role model." Sheila describes how her mentor would explain upcoming projects, even letting her take the relevant data and building the business case, staking a position, and making a recommendation. And she helped Sheila with all of this behind the scenes. "No risk, lots of rewards," Sheila says. One noteworthy incident was about whether the organization should expand into China. Sheila's mentor took the time to help her manage that strategic recommendation, which the company ultimately adopted. "She was a great example of how to develop women," Sheila says. "She hosted meals in her own home and really took the time to help me. Leadership takes time and investment. Now I pay that forward—not just with females but also males. We all need to create the next generation of leadership."

> **We all need to create the next generation of leadership.**

June didn't have the benefits that Sheila enjoyed with her mentor. Finding mentors was difficult for her. Early in her career, as she faced many challenges, she didn't have anyone to kick around ideas with or to get input from. She longed for a mentor. "Most senior leaders are busy and you have to be really creative in finding the ones that are truly willing to help you," she says. And there are larger issues as well that can challenge women to find the mentors they need. "Women encounter strongly biased cultures, as many men are also now afraid of mentoring women due to the #MeToo movement," June says. "You need to be persistent in asking for mentors and sometimes it helps with an official mentor program within the company, so both sides are comfortable with the mentor and mentee."

June feels fortunate to have been able to work with a few mentors and sponsors in her career. Today, she commits to mentoring as many other women in STEM as she can, demonstrating that just because you have challenges finding a mentor, that's not a reason not to be a mentor. To be a successful technical woman means taking on a mentoring role for the next generation of developing leaders. It might be the greatest legacy you can leave.

Developing Male Allies

Many companies that recognize the power of mentoring are now taking their mentoring programs even further. Some are even using mentoring to actively address second-generation gender bias (practices that appear the same for everyone but are created by men and inadvertently discriminate against women). For example, we know of an advertising technology company that launched a reverse mentoring program in which younger women mentored senior leadership to help them better understand what young women experience. They met three times for 45 to 60 minutes over several months to share stories about the challenges they faced, and during that time, hidden biases were revealed to their male colleagues that before were invisible to them.

One man who participated in that program told us that afterward he felt a heightened awareness of what it's like to work as a woman in a male-dominated industry. For example, he said that if he hadn't participated, he would not have noticed that one man on his team regularly interrupted women. As a result, he later pulled that man aside to reprimand him.

This man's heightened awareness prepared him to become what we call a "male ally". In STEM fields, the availability of and access to male allies can make a huge difference in the development and advancement of women through the ranks. Francesca, for example, tells us that male allies played major roles throughout her career and helped her get to where she is today. She remembers one particular incident, when she faced sexism during a meeting as a young, green investor with an all-male group. It was a male ally who stood up for her in that meeting.

"One of the older men in the meeting assumed I was an assistant and told me how he would like his coffee," she says. "My quick-witted partner said, 'The doctor also takes her coffee with milk,' and then went to get coffee for all of us." She thinks the episode embarrassed the older colleague, and she hopes he learned a lesson about making assumptions. "It was wonderful that my partner supported me, and we had a great working relationship after that," she says. "But it's really frustrating that he had to. In Europe (where Francesca's work is located), women continue to be mistaken for the tea lady no matter how senior you are."

Francesca had mentors who played a critical role throughout her career. These people were supportive of her goals and pushed her to achieve them. "My mentors, male and female, formal and informal, allowed me to think through the different options [of my career] and come up with new choices," she says. "Over the years, I have kept those relationships, and still reach out to them to get input on new ideas." As of this writing, Francesca is working with colleagues to create a women's leadership program.

It's worth noting that male allies don't always come in the form of supervisors; they can also be peers. When Deb was a senior researcher at a medical device company, she was given an opportunity to move into the company's innovation and venturing group—an incubator for new ideas. As a research fellow and director of new ventures, she would be responsible for leading the development of next-generation products. She felt it was a good fit because she had such deep expertise in the clinical areas that the group would be addressing.

Leaders at Deb's company wanted to give the leadership role to a director in the commercial team, a man with business experience but no technical background. Deb understood the clinical background and the product technologies but was told she didn't have the commercial background that the company thought was necessary. As a solution, Deb suggested that she and the other candidate be allowed to work together and jointly lead the initiative. That way, she could learn the commercial side from him, and he could learn the technical side from her. "It happened because I suggested the two of us would be significantly more powerful together than either one of us could be alone," Deb says. "I have made this a habit throughout my career: Find a person to team up with, a person who has complementary skills."

> "It happened because I suggested the two of us would be significantly more powerful together than either one of us could be alone," Deb says. "I have made this a habit throughout my career: Find a person to team up with, a person who has complementary skills."

Career Partners for Life

Male allies can be particularly beneficial to technical women when it comes to career advancement. Joy was working at a research and development center for exploration technology and feeling somewhat unfulfilled when she was contacted by a male ally from college who told her about a job at an aeronautics company he thought she'd be perfect for. The position was one she'd go on to hold for nearly a decade. Then, when Joy was working for another company, she saw a position that would be perfect for her colleague and hired him. And it didn't end there. Later, the colleague returned the favor and got her a job at another company he was working for. "We have been getting each other jobs for 20 years," she says. They remain friends and keep in touch.

Similarly, Chris's first manager at Xerox in the IT department helped advance her career. He was a major contributor to her success and set the tone for many of her relationships with male allies throughout her career. "During my first week on the job, he made appointments for me to meet with all of his direct reports and others I would be working with so that I could better understand their roles and how I would be working with them," she says. "He was really patient, sharing, and treated me well. When I was ready, he helped me get my next job on the corporate IT strategy team, which was quite a big step forward."

Despite the support Chris received from several male allies at different companies, she was no stranger to the sexism that often comes with working in the male-dominated tech industry. But she continued to benefit from male allies and credits one with helping her take on a new position that she never imagined she could handle. "Though most of the startups I've worked for in Silicon Valley have had the typical misogynist founders and 'good old boy' leadership teams, I've also had positive experiences," she says. Chris describes her work at a CRM startup where she was vice president of operations. "I was fortunate to work with a CEO who really believed that I had the potential to do more," she says. When the vice president of engineering left the company, Chris offered to help recruit a new one. But the CEO had other ideas. "He looked me in the eye," Chris says, "and said, 'I want you to do it.' I had never considered that I could lead that highly experienced team since I really didn't have software development expertise. But with such a strong vote of confidence from the CEO, I took it on. I learned what he already knew—leadership is more important than specific technical knowledge."

Male Allies Help Crash the Good Old Boys Party

Sheila is also familiar with the good old boys' network but has found male allies that help her maneuver around it. Once she understood how the system worked, she was able to bring like-minded men around to her point of view and present a united front that the "good old boys" didn't expect. "I would see the good old boys' network happening when major agreements and decisions occur outside of the meeting—in the 'inner sanctum' where women are not welcome. I have felt that my whole career—the real conversations don't always happen in the room. The guys get together and the actual meeting is perfunctory."

Sheila realized that not all men are included in the boys' club and found that some men, particularly those who are more introverted, aren't always invited to the inner sanctum. Throughout her career she's made these men her allies and works with them to accomplish her goals. "I team up with the other outsiders in advance and then we work together in the meeting to move the discussion in the other direction," Sheila says. "In one case, I was trying to get approval to put in a remote operating center to control operations in the mines. Some of the key guys who weren't supportive--I saw them grabbing coffee together, shooting the breeze, thick as thieves, getting ready to shut down my idea." But Sheila had other ideas—and other allies. She had prepared the data and rationale for an alternative viewpoint, and she worked with men outside of the boys' club in advance of the meeting

Observed progress when men are engaged in gender inclusion programs

- 96% — Men are engaged
- 30% — Men are not engaged

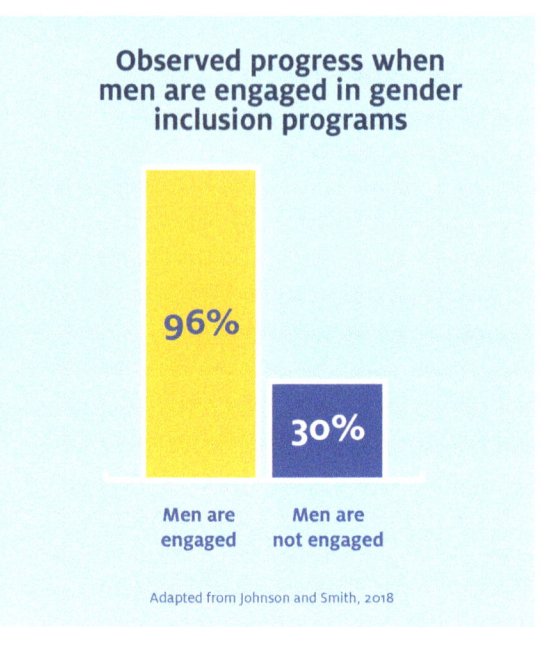

Adapted from Johnson and Smith, 2018

and they received approval. "The fact that I was very well-prepared and had my male supporters lined up really made the difference, "she says. "But women don't often build alliances like that, so they can't win. It's a must to get your ideas heard."

We have often seen this dynamic at work ourselves. I (Patty) led a breakout group session about women in venture capital at a conference on Corporate Venturing in January of 2018, amid the news about allegations of sexual harassment by Harvey Weinstein in Hollywood and Justin Caldbeck in Silicon Valley—home to many of the conference participants. I was surprised to see that session participants were primarily men. When I asked them why and what they were hoping to learn, there were two major questions: "What can we do to help?" and "Can we still have dinner meetings with women?" My answers were that if business is getting done at dinner, then include women. And, I added, becoming a male ally and mentor is one of the most important ways that men can help women succeed.

Male allies can do more than benefit women in male-dominated industries like tech. In a *Harvard Business Review* article, W. Brad Johnson and David Smith (2018) write: "Evidence shows that when men are deliberately engaged in gender inclusion programs, 96 percent of organizations see progress—compared to only 30 percent of organizations where men are not engaged."

When women are supported in the workplace, the benefits spread widely.

Takeaways, Tips, and Tools

- The use of a mentor at the beginning of a career can promote risk taking, which in turn encourages women to take on stretch assignments that accelerate their development. This dynamic is especially salient to women in STEM, who face obstacles specific to that field.

- The good old boys' club doesn't include all of the men in an organization. Those men who are not part of the network can be promising allies with technical women.

- Not even the best planned and resourced mentoring program will meet expectations if mentors aren't prepared to take on the responsibility or willing to make the commitment.

What You Can Do

In celebration of International Women's Day in 2018, CCL created a toolkit for supporting mentoring and sponsoring in organizations. Drawn from best practices across many organizations, the toolkit is available at ccl.org/mentoring-women. Here are a few of our favorite tactics from the toolkit.

> **Become familiar with what good mentors do.** Mentors who make a difference perform these five actions (they do more, but these five are key).
>
> ***See and assess opportunities and threats.*** Mentors help mentees explore the pros and cons of working on projects or pursuing new opportunities. They look for roles and projects that offer development, visibility, or good "press," and they help their mentees identify potential allies, resources, or shifting circumstances. They also stay alert for

97

emerging conflicts, potential adversaries, organizational system complications, and potentially difficult organizational changes.

Guide, counsel, and coach. Mentors are confidants, sounding boards, and personal advisors. They may address leadership skills and behaviors and help mentees explore and understand emotional reactions, relationships, and organizational culture. They may or may not address personal factors, such as life stage or non-work commitments or problems.

Teach. Mentors transfer their knowledge, teach skills, and share their experiences. They may invite the mentee to shadow them on a project or join them in meetings, then debrief the experience later. They may also do the reverse: shadow the mentee and provide feedback on what they observe.

Model. Mentors are willing to discuss how they handle situations, as well as their ethics, values, standards, and methods. Mentees pick up many things through observation and will likely follow the mentor's lead, adapting what they see to their own style and situation.

Motivate and inspire. Mentors support, validate, and encourage their mentees. They engage corroboratively and build on ideas, rather than claim authority and issue directives. They help their mentee link her values, aspirations, hopes, needs, and passions to her developmental goals or organizational agenda.

Set expectations in mentoring relationships. Talk to your mentor about expectations and plan to reassess them periodically. This is especially important when men are mentoring across gender or other differences. Clarifying expectations can be helpful for knowing how to interact with one another during the relationship. Some things to discuss:

The purpose of the mentoring relationship. From the start, agreement on purpose will focus the relationship on results and process. You and your mentor can get at those aspects of the relationship with questions such as:

- What is the mentee currently working on?
- What are their goals, challenges, aspirations, and interests?
- Does the mentor have helpful knowledge, experience, opportunities, or connections to share that relate to these goals, challenges, or interests?
- How might the organization benefit from your conversations with each other?

Agree to norms. Whether the mentoring relationship is initiated by the mentee or the mentor, both should ask clarifying questions, such as:

- How often and where will you meet?
- Who will initiate the meetings?
- What type of guidance would be helpful?
- Which topics are confidential?
- How long might this relationship last?
- Are there any other goals or expectations?

Identify potential problems and plan how to address them. No relationship, even developmental ones based on trust and purpose, is free from friction all the time. Consider and discuss concerns, for example:

Are either of you concerned about not having enough time to get together? If so, decide whether it might make more sense to arrange shorter, more frequent meetings, rather than longer, less frequent appointments.

Even with the best of intentions, men may harbor conscious and unconscious biases that impact how they work with women. According to W. Brad Johnson and David Smith, the authors of *Athena Rising: How and Why Men Should Mentor Women*, the following biases (and more) "have the potential to undermine women and poison...mentoring efforts:"

- Women lack sufficient drive and career commitment; they don't possess the ambition to make it.
- Women will eventually leave to have children; they're a risky investment.
- Women are overcommitted outside of work; they're too busy being wives and mothers to be productive and get promoted.

What will your mentor do if you don't ask for help or seem unreceptive to feedback?

What will you do if the mentor doesn't provide help or relevant support?

What if this developmental match isn't the best fit?

What Organizations Can Do

Double down on mentoring. Ensure that mentoring practices follow guidelines for inclusion and diversity. Focus on career transition points. The biggest challenge we see is establishing clear processes, and providing the right level of training and support, as well as pathways to change mentoring relationships that aren't working out.

Get creative. Senior leaders have busy agendas. Seek ways to optimize their time for contribution by involving them in targeted ERG meetings, panels, and small gatherings where they can spend focused time with select groups they can take time to know.

- Women who work as many-or more-hours than men are aberrant; they should be home tending to children and spouse.

- Women don't have the leadership traits necessary to succeed; they're not assertive, competitive, or stoic enough.

- Women are too emotional; they lack the mental toughness required to lead.

- Strong women are b*****s; strong men are leaders.

From Johnson and Smith, 2016, p. 57.

GENERATION NEXT

It's May 2019 in the Marriott conference center in Austin, Texas. Heather Quinn, an IEEE WIE (Women in Engineering) board member and senior scientist at the Los Alamos National Laboratory, hosts a packed room for a resilience yoga break. Fully dressed women in business attire find their way into triangle poses. The hallways buzz with voices. The voices carry stories.

Stories of perseverance, of pride, of camaraderie, of competition, of exclusion, of allies. Stories of girls pursuing their fascination with science and math. Stories of women rising to senior positions in organizations, expanding their formidable technical know-how into organizational insights on strategy, customers, and innovation. Stories that in a small part we tried to capture in this book. Technical women have stories to tell. The lessons of experience are bound up in those stories. Now that we're talking, and listening, it's time to ask: What's next?

Generational Pathways

It's not unusual to find multiple generations at work in contemporary organizations. Stories in the popular press often highlight generational differences for any number of reasons. Sometimes it's to explain behavior (Gen Z socializes through screens). Sometimes it's to reinforce stereotypes (Boomers ruined the world). Sometimes it's to appear clever (every Millennial has a shelf of participation trophies at home).

The way of work and the world don't neatly conform to the ideas we have of them. Actual behavior often reveals that while different generations respond to the world differently, the differences shrink when you realize that, for the most part, they want the same things. Differences become visible because the context within which different generations live informs their beliefs and beliefs influence action (Deal & Levenson, 2016). Many of the women we interviewed for this book were pioneers in technical fields. They are predominantly Gen Xers or Baby Boomers. The barriers they faced remain but have come under the pressure of a new wave of technical women who don't often practice go-along-to-get-along patience.

"The best thing about young women coming up is that they don't have the voice in their head that tells them they don't deserve to be here," Chris says. Younger technical women are unwilling to accommodate attitudes of men that support the biases of a field dominated by men. "They are demanding a seat at the table" she continues. "They demand salary transparency, bonuses and raises distributed fairly—all things that we never had the guts to actually demand. Older white men seem bemused and don't know how to take it. But they better get used to it."

> "Older white men seem bemused and don't know how to take it. But they better get used to it."

Heather (whom we met in chapter one) echoes Chris's perspective. She talks about how Millennial women don't put up with displays of inequity behavior in the workplace. "The younger generation won't put up with some of the things that we did, and with the shortage of engineers, particularly females, they don't have to," she says.

Generational Flows

A technical woman's journey doesn't flow in one direction. As younger women move forward, the women who came before them, if they are wise, look back to see what they can learn from the incoming generations of technical women. "I learn from Millennials every day," says Sabina. "Working with them has been a turning point in my confidence. I used to cover it up when I didn't know something, now I am more confident admitting what I don't know and getting input and knowledge from others. Millennials are so much more transparent, more activist. I think that skipped my generation."

June shares Sabina's gratitude for the lessons that younger women bring to the STEM organizations. "Millennials are much more open, confident, more relaxed, more entrepreneurial," she says. "They're not as stressed about climbing the corporate ladder. They're also more supportive of women." The latest generation of women beginning STEM careers come with perspectives shaped by liberation and social justice movements, by #MeToo rebellions against male privilege (especially the most egregious manifestations as sexual harassment and assault), and by cultural shifts in educational access. "What makes this generation [Millennials] stand out is the context they live in, more than that they are different as people," says Jennifer Deal, coauthor of *What Millennials Want from Work* (2016). "Speaking truth to power around diversity means something different now than it did 20 years ago."

That's not to say that it's a perfect world. Far from it. But the responses to it are different. When I (Kelly) returned to the U.S. tech sector in 2014, more than 12 years after leaving that situation and moving overseas, I was surprised and disappointed by the lack of advancement of technical women during that time. The exclusion of technical women from roles and responsibilities and other aspects of STEM workplaces was still evident in those cultures.

Culture changes when the practices that continually recreate it change. We count four aspects of practice that can help STEM fields advance toward inclusion. Action is needed on all four fronts. They work in complementary ways to advance a culture that is both receptive to inclusion of all genders and more diverse—with all the benefits possible in that environment.

Dialogue Drives Diversity

When Elizabeth Brown from Unity Technology stood before an audience at the 2018 Diversity and Inclusion conference in San Francisco, she challenged them: "What should you do if you see gender discriminatory behavior at work?" A pregnant pause. Murmurs spread throughout the room: "Tell HR." That was a comfortable and common reply. "Really?" she asked. She wasn't going to let them off that easy.

As chief people officer of a global enterprise with more than 2000 employees in more than 20 locations, Brown brings far more workplace diversity challenges to her office than any HR team can handle alone. "Our job in HR," she continues, "is to help employees become responsible for upholding and enforcing our culture of inclusion." That's a big ask.

> "Our job in HR, she continues, "is to help employees become responsible for upholding and enforcing our culture of inclusion." That's a big ask.

Policy enactment, while critical and foundational, isn't enough. Inclusion or exclusion are lived experiences. Shifting perspectives asks us to experience empathy for another's experience. To put it into action requires dialogue. We need to talk. We need to tell our stories. We need to listen.

Brown tells a story of a 30-minute workshop keying off this question: "What do you do when someone says something sexual?" Table talk inevitably ensues. There is some uncomfortable shifting around in chairs. "What could you say to address someone who is showing that behavior to a colleague of yours?" Table groups brainstorm. Brown runs these exercises and follows with email reminders of accountability. All to drive Unity toward an inclusive culture.

Jamil Zaki, director of the Stanford Social Neuroscience Lab, has looked at the different ways people can be programmed to be empathetic. On a recent episode of Hidden Brain, Zaki explained an experiment conducted in the UK. Manchester United fans were asked to write about their passion for the renowned football team (or soccer team, to those of us in the United States). When the fans left the lab, they encountered an injured athlete (an actor played the role). When the actor wore a Manchester United jersey, the fans attended to him quickly. When he wore the rival team Liverpool's jersey, they ignored him. Another population of participants were asked to write about their passion for the sport of football. They encountered the same actor in the street but behaved differently from the first group. This time, they helped him, independent of the jersey he wore. The experiment illustrates how easily we identify with one group. "The key," says Jamil, "is to expand our view so that our perspective is of a larger group." Dialogue plays an important role in that expansion.

Women's Groups and Executive Sponsorship

At an aerospace company where we conducted the Advancing Technical Women leadership program, we held a dinner with the women participants and the senior-most scientists in the organization. The STEM women had dedicated time to meet and engage in informal conversation with the executive leaders. The responses of the senior scientists in the group surprised us: "I never knew this person and was surprised that her name had not been brought to my attention," was a common remark. "We have a lot of work to do, it seems, to increase the percentage of women in senior roles," remarked another. There were no comments against inclusion. That organization continues to grow its efforts to develop STEM women, leveraging executive involvement as it does so.

During one executive panel we attended at another women's leadership program, a woman called out to the mostly male panel, "Would you say there is a glass ceiling here?" After a very long silence, the lone woman in the panel replied, "Yes." The room fell silent for a very long moment, and then the executives and women participants engaged in deeper dialogue. Woe be to leaders who sit at a panel on diversity and are not prepared to have their thinking challenged. Acknowledging the issue, followed by continued steps toward retention and promotion of women, is key. In this case, that conversation was an important first step.

As we've witnessed from the women's stories told in this book, strong communication skills and a thick skin are important when engaging in these conversations about diversity. They require well-honed listening skills and a level of comfort with being vulnerable, open, and curious. Such conversations aren't practiced by STEM workers nearly as often as rational and complex problem solving. Technology companies have noticed the difference and are working to develop conversation skills among their workforces. Focused learning and practice with effective communication has to be threaded into any inclusive dialogue process.

5% away from the tipping point of sustainability.

5%

25%

Networks, Advocacy and the Ripple Effect

Here's a number: 25. That's the percentage of women who are currently employed in science, technology, engineering and mathematics (STEM) in the United Kingdom, according to the WISE campaign.

Helen Wollaston, chief executive of the WISE Campaign says, "Having seen the number of women in core STEM roles reach our target of 1 million, we now need to keep up the momentum and aim for a target of 30% of women in STEM which is critical mass for sustainability." But if we haven't reached that number, as the WISE report suggests, what makes it possible

> "I've helped myself, now I will help a colleague."

that it will be reached anytime soon? Part of the answer lies in the growing power of personal networks, particularly among younger women.

Once a woman finds a way to advance her STEM career and persist through adversity, she is equipped to help someone else. Women who tap into their own sense of identity, their ability to develop a strategic network with support, sponsors, and access to challenging work can be resource—nodes in the personal networks that lead to the tipping point: "I've helped myself, now I will help a colleague."

With strong advocacy by women, a sustainable pipeline of STEM women in leadership roles can be developed. Used in combination with dialogue and the support of women's groups, the possibility of exponential change moves closer to reality.

Inclusive Practices and Technologies

Research has shown that an unconscious gender bias leads to the hiring of men over women when comparing identical resumes. But when gender is removed from the resume, and prior to face to face interviews, the probability of selection of women versus men becomes equal (Carnes, Geller, Fine, Sheridan, & Handelsman, 2005).

Women are less likely than men to apply for a promotion if they do not feel they meet job requirements (Sandberg, 2013). That's evident in STEM and other roles. Organizations should examine how they specify job requirements and encourage persons of all genders to apply.

While current artificial intelligence harbors a bias against women, technology does have the potential to be used to improve diversity and inclusion. One example involves the use of virtual reality (VR) to promote empathy. People who saw in virtual reality what it would be like to lose their jobs and homes developed longer-lasting compassion toward the homeless compared with those people who used different media, like text, to explore the same situation (Becoming Homeless: A Human Experience, 2018). What that means is that VR's ability to put people in different scenarios significantly impacts people's degree of empathy and can shift their perspectives.

Takeaways, Tips, and Tools

- Multiple generations in the workforce make it possible for "reverse mentoring" where more senior technical women can learn from millennial and younger generations of women.

- Achieving organizational diversity requires open dialogue in which ambivalence is allowed—sometimes a challenge for STEM workers of all genders given their usual propensity for precision and single solutions to vexing problems.

- Women who build and sustain successful STEM careers are in a position to develop other women to deal with obstacles and take more senior roles in STEM workplaces.

What You Can Do

We have seen women move beyond their functional role and start developing women during workplace STEM events. They sign up to mentor others and seek more prominent community roles. You have many avenues for advancing this movement. It's not an empty gesture. It does help. Identify the range of options available to you right now. Choose actions that align with your values and aspirations. We offer the following as tactics that STEM women can apply to their experiences.

> **Write your own narrative.** Connect with your own values, beliefs, and passions to fuel your career. The only way your employer can help give you a challenging work project that perfectly fits your goals is if you have first recognized what your values, beliefs, and passions are. For some women, this may take focused reflection. It can help to engage with trusted others who have a good perspective on who you are as a person and agree to provide feedback or insight that may help deepen your self-awareness. They can also help you find the words to express your values so that colleagues, bosses, and others can understand.

> **Explore your own bias and strengthen your empathy muscles.** You have biases, whatever your gender. Neuroscience researchers have conducted many studies on the topic of implicit bias, and basically, biases are impossible to avoid (Hart, Whalen, Shin, McInerney, Fischer, & Rauch, 2000). Recognize the ground you're standing on. Humans carry and use biases all the time but when those biases slip into prejudice or exclusion, they become real problems. The best way to become more inclusive is to first accept that bias is human. Once you have accepted that, you can extend empathy toward people with whom you disagree. Get curious about your own biases. What are they? How do you see things differently from others? What does that tell you?

> **Speak truth to bias and support others.** On a flight from San Diego to San Jose, I (Kelly) sat next to a Silicon Valley company technical executive. He observed me working on documentation of the Advancing Technical Women's program and initiated a discussion. "Let me tell you a story that

just happened last week," he began. He went on to explain how, during a meeting, a direct report of his was presenting to the team on a topic, and was repeatedly interrupted by her male colleagues. "She is this diminutive Chinese woman who is smart as a whip, though a bit soft-spoken, and it really enraged me to see them cutting her off," he said. He told me that he stopped the meeting to give feedback to the colleagues who were interrupting her.

Have you turned the other way when observing gender bias at your workplace? All of us—technical women and the men who work with them—should take it upon ourselves to go beyond their company's mandatory harassment training. It's important that we speak out when we see biased behavior, and if possible, give direct feedback to the instigator about behavior we observed and its impact on us.

What about Men?

When facilitating a CCL Advancing Technical Women program, it's not unusual for us to hear that male colleagues and bosses also want to attend. It's an appetite that can't be explained only by the program's focus on STEM. Nor can it be explained only by the program's highlighting the developmental journey of women in the field as they look toward taking on senior roles in their organizations. Men have access to similar developmental experiences. What's behind the appetite to attend what is ostensibly a special experience for women?

Perhaps one answer lies in the intersection of STEM, leadership, and gender. How are men—at least the ones expressing interest in Advancing Technical Women—to understand how women negotiate that intersection? How do they hear and learn to understand their stories? How might they learn how to interact with women in unbiased ways? The first step: Listen to their stories.

Stories are a window on experience. They spur empathy and, in the best case, awareness and commitment. As women who share the experience of working in a field dominated by men, we admit to disappointment and anger when stories come to light of biased behavior, from unintentional slights to crude jokes to outright harassment. The stories we pass on in these pages open a window to what a successful STEM career for women can look like and how it can be built despite bias. We believe many men want to hear those stories.

Temper your stance against bias by practicing tolerance for the different life paths people have taken, what they have learned, and what has been ingrained in them during their journeys. Tolerance doesn't mean automatic acceptance. It means only that you recognize the humanity of others and are mindful of that as you bring colleagues to a more inclusive viewpoint. You still must expose biases. You also must help make change.

Find your unique way to be a catalyst. It is the closing session of the first ever Advancing Technical Woman's program. Women in attendance were responding to this question: "What are you going to do to expand this experience beyond the group in this room?" Some women say they want to sponsor the next group of women planning to go through the program. Other women say they were going to be more active in their company's women-in-STEM employee resource group. Within minutes, the 25 women present proposed ways of engaging at least 100 more women and with executive stakeholders.

What Organizations Can Do

Building a talent pipeline of women in STEM through adequate mentorship, sponsorship, and equity in hiring and promotion processes requires buy-in on the part of managers right up through the C-Suite. Research done by McKinsey and company illustrates that sustained impact requires executive involvement. We have learned through research and interaction with EDI executives in Fortune 500 companies that holding senior executives accountable for progress in diversity initiatives enables those initiatives to be effective. In at least one organization we spoke with, senior executives have a percentage of their bonus dependent upon sustaining a diversity quota. Organizations that make this effort, even by providing financial incentives, will receive the upside benefits over time that a diverse workforce brings. Once the top of the organization is engaged, they need to continue to push this down through the organization and sustain that effort over enough time so that a significant shift in both diversity and organizational culture can take place.

Beating the Odds

We are thankful to the generations of women in STEM who preceded us and who will follow us. Our predecessors blazed trails and carved out a small space for us and other technical women to find our paths into STEM careers. Our successors remind us of the necessity for inclusion and fairness in work. We are and remain mindful that there are many workplace stories other than those of technical women. Many women work in jobs and take on careers without the shield, as thin as it might be, of "engineer" attached to their names. We fully acknowledge the situation of many women in the workforce outside of STEM—often one of less pay, less respect, less power. It's beyond the scope of this book to wrestle with the deeply entangled subject of cultural bias and inequity and reach a conclusion and derive a course of action. It's our hope that technical women feel solidarity with women in other professions and in other labor forces. The stories they might share across the lines of personal history and economic borders can only enrich us all.

The number of women in STEM is growing but still lags in relation to the percentage of men. Celebrate the curiosity of young girls and accomplished rocket scientists. Embrace your dream. Avoid the trap of prejudice, the suggestion that girls aren't as good as boys in science and math. And when you make it into whatever organization values your talents, bring along a nose for business, which differentiates the people at the top of organizations. The strength of robust technical knowledge can become a weakness when overused.

Working as a woman in a STEM career and securing your place in the field isn't for the faint of heart. You are a single yet significant part of transforming the culture in which you work. If you draw any lesson from the stories related in this book, let it be that it's possible to beat the odds and create a career in the field you love.

We have heard about and experienced ourselves the reality that has faced women in STEM since the first day they entered the field. Marie Curie, the first woman granted a Nobel in physics (she was granted another in Chemistry) is rightfully recognized for her accomplishments. But she was hardly an exception to bias. Her 1903 Nobel came to her only after the mathematician Magnus Goesta Mittag-Leffler interceded. The original nomination addressed Henri Becquerel (who accidentally discovered radiation) and Pierre Curie, Marie's husband and lab partner. In the popular press of the time she was generally portrayed as Pierre Curie's helpmate. He certainly knew better.

From the words of the women we spoke to, we want to show the ways women have triumphed over the challenges of overt bias and the times that they haven't been able to. We have seen how women move through hurdles seen by some and not by others because of their competitive spirit, determination, perseverance, and resilience. We salute them, and are excited to see what changes this new decade will bring.

REFERENCES

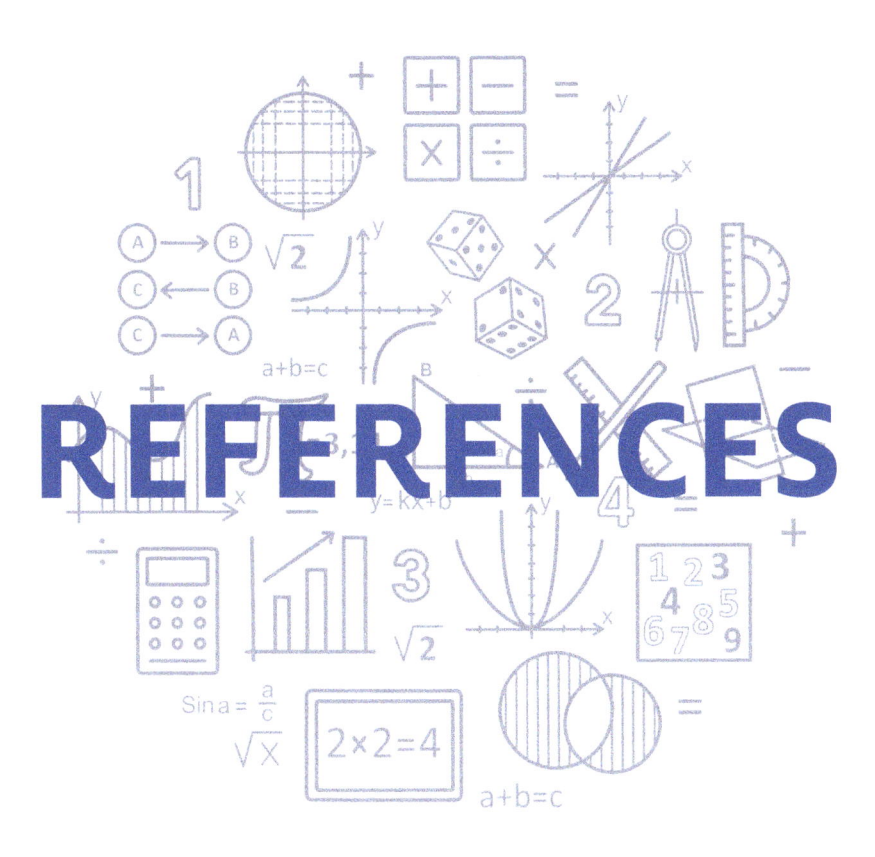

Ashcraft, C., McLain, B., & Eger, E. (2016). *Women in tech: The facts, 2016 update*. Boulder, CO: National Center for Women & Information Technology in partnership with NCWIT Workforce Alliance.

Becoming Homeless: A Human Experience [Computer software]. (2018). Stanford, CT: Virtual Human Interaction Lab.

Bhatti, R. (2019, July 19). With 'mission mangal' trailer out, here's a look at the women who put India on mars. Retrieved November 12, 2019, from https://www.scoopwhoop.com/women/meet-the-women-scientists-behind-mangalyaan-india-s-maiden-mission-to-mars/

Bureau of Labor Statistics. (2018). "Table 11: Employed persons by detailed occupation, sex, race, and hispanic or latino ethnicity," Current Population Survey, Household Data Annual Averages 2017. Retrieved from https://www.bls.gov/cps/cpsaat11.htm

Carnes, M., Geller, S., Fine, E., Sheridan, J., & Handelsman, J. (2005). NIH director's pioneer awards: Could the selection process be biased against women? Journal of Women's Health, 14(8), 684–691. https://doi.org/10.1089/jwh.2005.14.684

Chawla, D. S. (2019, Nov. 1). In decision certain to draw fire, journal will publish heavily criticized paper on gender differences in physics. Science, 66(6466). Retrieved from https://www.sciencemag.org/news/2019/11/decision-certain-draw-fire-journal-will-publish-heavily-criticized-paper-gender

Chernin, P. (Producer), & Melfi, T. (Director). (2016). *Hidden figures* [Motion picture]. United States. Fox 2000 Pictures.

Clerkin, C. (2017). *What women want—And why you want women—In the workplace*. Greensboro, NC: Center for Creative Leadership and Watermark.

Clerkin, C. (2019). The role of respect and identity in retaining women engineers. Unpublished manuscript, Center for Creative Leadership, Greensboro, NC, USA.

Colantuono, S. (2016, Feb. 4). There are 3 keys to career success—But women are only taught 2 of them. Time. Retrieved from https://time.com/4167912/career-advice-women/

Cole, S., Riccio, M., & Balcetis, E. (2014). Focused and fired up: Narrowed attention produces perceived proximity and increases goal-relevant action. *Motivation and Emotion*, 38(6), 815-822.

Corbett, C., & Hill, C. (2015). *Solving the equation: the variables for women's success in engineering and computing.* Washington, DC: AAUW.

Csikszentmihalyi, M. (1990). *Flow: The psychology of optimal experience.* New York, NY: Harper and Row.

Cullen, K. L., Palus, C. J., & Appaneal, C. (2014). *Developing network perspective: Understanding the basics of social networks and their role in leadership* [White paper] Greensboro, NC: Center for Creative Leadership.

Deal, J. J., & Levenson, A. (2016). *What millennials want from work: How to maximize engagement in today's workforce.* New York: McGraw-Hill.

Dweck, C. S. (2006). *Mindset: The new psychology of success.* New York: Random House.

Fernández-Aráoz, C. (2014). 21st-century talent spotting. *Harvard Business Review*. 92. 46-54, 56, 138. Retrieved from https://search.ebscohost.com/login.aspx?direct=true&db=plh&AN=96090576&site=ehost-live

Ganley C.M., George C. E., Cimpian J. R., Makowski M.B. (2018).

Gender equity in college majors: Looking beyond the STEM/non-STEM dichotomy for answers regarding female participation. *American Educational Research Journal*, 55(3), 453-487. https://doi.org/10.3102/0002831217740221

Geekgirl. (n.d.). Retrieved November 7, 2019, from http://geekgirl.com.au/blog

Glass, J. L., Sassler, S., Levitte, Y., & Michelmore, K. M. (2013). What's so special about STEM? A comparison of women's retention in STEM and professional occupations. *Social Forces*, 92(2), 723-756. Retrieved from https://www.ncbi.nlm.nih.gov/pmc/articles/PMC4279242/

Goldsmith, M. (2014). *What got you here won't get you there*. New York, NY: MJF Books.

Gurvis, J., McCauley, C., & Swofford, M. (2016). Putting experience at the center of talent management [White paper]. Greensboro, NC: Center for Creative Leadership. Retrieved from https://www.ccl.org/articles/white-papers/putting-experience-center-talent-management/

Hallenbeck, G. (2016). *Learning agility: Unlock the lessons of experience*. Greensboro, NC: Center for Creative Leadership.

Halpern, D. F. (2004). A cognitive process taxonomy for sex differences in cognitive abilities. *Current Directions in Psychological Science*, 13(4), 135-139. https://doi.org/10.1111/j.0963-7214.2004.00292.x

Hart, A. J., Whalen, P. J., Shin, L. M., McInerney, S. C., Fischer, H., Rauch, S. L. (2000). Differential response in the human amygdala to racial outgroup vs. ingroup face stimuli. *NeuroReport* 11(11), 2351-2355. https://dx.doi.org/10.1097/00001756-200008030-00004

Hill, C., Corbett, C., & St. Rose, A. (2010). *Why so few? Women in science, technology, engineering, and mathematics.* Washington, DC: AAUW. Retrieved from https://www.aauw.org/files/2013/02/Why-So-Few-Women-in-Science-Technology-Engineering-and-Mathematics.pdf

Huang, J., Krivkovich, A., Starikova, I., Yee, L., & Zanoschi, D. (2019). *Women in the workplace 2019.* Retrieved from https://www.mckinsey.com/featured-insights/gender-equality/women-in-the-workplace-2019

Johnson, W. B., & Smith, D. (2016). *Athena rising: How and why men should mentor women.* Brookline, MA: Bibliomotion.

Johnson, W. B., & Smith, D. G. (2018, October 12). How men can become better allies to women. *Harvard Business Review.* Retrieved from https://hbr.org/2018/10/how-men-can-become-better-allies-to-women

Junger, S. (2016). *Tribe: On homecoming and belonging.* New York: Twelve/Hatchett Book Group.

Kane, J.M., & Mertz, J. E. (2012). Debunking myths about gender and mathematics performance. *Notices of the American Mathematica Society*, 51(1).

Kaplan, R. S., & Norton, D. P. (2001). *The strategy-focused organization: How balanced scorecard companies thrive in the new business environment.* Boston: Harvard Business School Press.

Kawasaki, G. (1990). *The macintosh way.* Glenview, IL: Scott, Foresman and Company.

Leavy, S. (2018). Gender bias in artificial intelligence: The need for diversity and gender Theory in machine learning. *Proceedings of the 1st International Workshop on Gender Equality in Software Engineering*, 14–16. https://doi.org/10.1145/3195570.3195580

Mac, R. (2019, June 12). "This picture featuring 15 tech men and 2 women looked doctored. The women were photoshopped in." Retrieved from https://www.buzzfeednews.com/article/ryanmac/tech-titans-women-fake-photoshop-cucinelli-gq

Mahdaoui, M. (2016, March 8). How far are we from gender equality in STEM? Retrieved from https://www.totaljobs.com/insidejob/gender-equality-in-stem/

Martineau, J., & Mount, P. (2018). *Kick some glass: 10 ways women succeed at work on their own terms.* New York: McGraw-Hill.

McBride, J. (2018, October 20). "Nobel laureate Donna Strickland: 'I see myself as a scientist, not a woman in science.'" *The Guardian.* Retrieved from www.theguardian.com/science/2018/oct/20/nobel-laureate-donna-strickland-i-see-myself-as-a-scientist-not-a-woman-in-science.

McCauley, C.D. (2006). *Developmental assignments: Creating learning experiences without changing jobs.* Greensboro, NC. Center for Creative Leadership.

National Science Board. (2016). Science and Engineering Indicators 2016. Arlington, VA: National Science Foundation (NSB-2016-1). Retrieved from https://www.nsf.gov/statistics/2016/nsb20161/#/downloads/report

Noonan, R. (2017) *Women in STEM: 2017 update.* Washington, D.C.: U.S. Department of Commerce. Retrieved Oct. 2019 from https://www.commerce.gov/news/fact-sheets/2017/11/women-stem-2017-update

Nugent, J. S., Pollack, A., & Travis, D. T. (2016). *The day-to-day experiences of workplace inclusion and exclusion.* New York: Catalyst. Retrieved from https://www.catalyst.org/research/the-day-to-day-experiences-of-workplace-inclusion-and-exclusion/

Oral-History: Anita Borg. (2001). Retrieved October 30, 2019, from Engineering and Technology History Wiki website: https://ethw.org/Oral-History:Anita_Borg

Orser, B., Riding, A., & Stanley, J. (2011). Perceived career challenges and response strategies of women in the advanced technology sector. *Entrepreneurship & Regional Development*, 24(1-2), 73–93. https://doi.org/10.1080/08985626.2012.637355

Ramsey, N. & McCorduck, P. (2005). *Where are the women in information technology*? University of Colorado, Boulder.

Rickard, K., & Crowther, A. (2015). The slower track: women in the STEM professions survey report. *Professionals Australia*. Retrieved from http://www.professionalsaustralia.org.au/professional-women/wp-content/uploads/sites/48/2014/03/2015-Women-in-the-STEM-Professions-Survey-Report.pdf

Ridley, J. (2018, October 2). Physics professor acts like a sexist pig at the best time imaginable. Retrieved March 19, 2019, from https://nypost.com/2018/10/02/physics-professor-acts-like-a-sexist-pig-at-the-best-time-imaginable/

Roger, D., & Petrie, N. (2016). *Work without stress: Building a resilient mindset for lasting success*. New York: McGraw-Hill Education.

Sandberg, S. (2013). *Lean in: Women, work, and the will to lead*. New York: Alfred A. Knopf.

Simard, C., Henderson, A. D., Gilmartin, S. K., Schiebinger L., & Whitney, T. (2008). *Climbing the technical ladder: Obstacles and solutions for mid-*

level women in technology. Stanford: CA: Michelle R. Clayman Institute for Gender Research, Stanford University, Anita Borg Institute for Women and Technology.

Stewart, A. (2019, July 25). Why is artificial intelligence biased against women? Retrieved from http://www.hrtechnologist.com/articles/diversity/why-is-artificial-intelligence-biased-against-women/

Thompson, B. (2016, May 28). Take a tip from Bezos: Customers always need a seat at the table. *Entrepreneur*. Retrieved November 2, 2019, from https://www.entrepreneur.com/article/234254

Wang, M. T., & Degol, J. L. (2017). Gender gap in science, technology, engineering, and mathematics (STEM): Current knowledge, implications for practice, policy, and future directions. *Educational Psychology Review*, 29(1), 119-140. https://doi.org/10.1007/s10648-015-9355-x

Williams, K. (2018). *Women in tech: How to attract and retain top talent*. Indeed Blog. Retrieved from http://blog.indeed.com/2018/11/06/women-in-tech-report/

Williams, Heidi, et al. (2018). Elevating women in tech: Why mentoring matters. Retrieved from www.geteverwise.com/webinar/on-demand/women-in-tech-why-mentoring-matters-deck.pdf

WISE (n.d.). *WISE says UK needs 30% of women in core STEM as it publishes its annual analysis of ONS data*. WISE campaign. https://www.wisecampaign.org.uk/news/wise-says-uk-needs-30-of-women-in-core-stem-as-it-publishes-its-annual-analysis-of-ons-data/

ABOUT THE AUTHORS

Patty is an Innovation and Venture Catalyst with the Center for Creative Leadership, focused on leadership trends and new service innovation. Prior to joining CCL, she was an innovation and corporate venture capital consultant working with venture capitalists, startups, and global corporations. She was previously VP Marketing at Symantec and at start-up Ramp Networks where she led marketing and corporate positioning strategy from product introduction to NASDAQ IPO and acquisition. Patty was an instructor for CalTech Industrial Relations and advisor to entrepreneurial programs at California College of the Arts/Design MBA and San Jose State University Lucas College and Graduate School of Business. Patty has a Bachelor of Arts from the University of Texas at Austin and currently resides in San Jose, California.

Kelly is the Global Portfolio leader for the Center for Creative Leadership, focusing on executive leadership and working with clients around the world. Kelly has lived globally and held associate faculty roles at EADA Business School in Barcelona, Spain, as well as consulted with global companies in the area of leadership and organizational development. She authored the book chapter, "Seeing teams as Human Systems" in the 2011 publication of "Do you Work or Collaborate?" ("¿Trabajas o colaboras?") by Profit Editorial, Spain. Prior to that, Kelly worked for Hewlett Packard as a manufacturing engineer and lead global manufacturing projects across the Americas and Asia. She has a Bachelor of Science in Mechanical Engineering from the University of California Davis and a Masters degree in Organizational and Executive Development from EADA, Spain. She currently resides in San Diego, California.

ABOUT CCL WOMEN'S LEADERSHIP

Advancing Technical Women

Advancing Technical Women was developed to help organizations recruit, retain, and promote women in STEM. Research shows that more women are entering technical fields, yet they are not advancing to the next levels of leadership at the expected rate. Based on the Center for Creative Leadership's decades of research on the leadership challenges of women, this program helps women take ownership of their careers and get prepared and energized to drive improved results for their teams and organizations. Using real-world experiential exercises and candid peer feedback, Advancing Technical Women helps women recognize and communicate their distinctive value with clarity and confidence while giving them research-based strategies and tools to help advance their careers.

Designed for high-potential women in STEM, participants learn to become skilled advocates and agents for their careers, transform personal attributes and strengths into a recognizable 'brand', build strategic networks that improve visibility and promotability, secure and succeed at challenging stretch assignments, improve communication skills and presence, and develop action plans empowering them to reach their career goals.

Advancing Technical Women was developed by Kelly Simmons and launched in 2018 after extensive piloting in Silicon Valley and at CCL headquarters in Greensboro, NC. Thousands of women have participated in Advancing Technical Women globally since then, often in conjunction with broader women's leadership and diversity initiatives. See www.ccl.org/atw

Women's Leadership Experience

CCL's Women's Leadership Experience is a multi-phased three-month development engagement designed to equip women who are already proven leaders with the knowledge and skills needed to have greater impact and broader influence within their organizations. The program is designed for women with upper-management and leadership experience. Admission to the Open Enrollment program is by application only, but many organizations chose to offer the customized Experience as part of broader diversity initiatives.

Participants gain clarity on how others perceive them as a leader and develop behaviors that support their personal leadership style, credibility, brand and career direction. They will also learn influence-building, strategic thinking, managing up and across the organization, navigating complex relationships, negotiation skills, and how to build and leverage strategic networks. Most importantly, women wil develop a career direction action plan and implement a personal leadership strategy.

The 3-month, multi-phased program deepens learning through ongoing peer relationships and provides the opportunity to develop a rich peer support network. The program also includes two 1:1 executive coaching sessions tailored to each participant. The gender-specific format allows for greater openness in a supportive environment and addresses the unique issues women face. The Women's Leadership Experience is highly experiential, allowing time for new skills & behaviors to be explored in a safe environment. See www.ccl.org/wle

ABOUT CCL

The Center for Creative Leadership® (CCL) is a top-ranked, global provider of leadership development. By leveraging the power of leadership to drive results that matter most to clients, CCL transforms individual leaders, teams, organizations, and society. Our array of cutting-edge solutions is steeped in extensive research and experience gained from working with hundreds of thousands of leaders at all levels. Ranked among the world's top providers of executive education by the Financial Times, CCL has locations in countries worldwide.